Jewish Sects
at the
Time of Jesus

MARCEL SIMON

Translated by
JAMES H. FARLEY

FORTRESS PRESS   PHILADELPHIA

This book is a translation of *Les sectes juives au temps de Jésus*, published by Presses universitaires de France in 1960.

Library of Congress Catalog Card Number 66-25265
ISBN 0-8006-0183-1

Second printing 1980

8283E80   Printed in the United States of America   1-183

Translator's Preface

IT IS A COMMONPLACE to claim that a book will fill a void in a particular field, but *Jewish Sects at the Time of Jesus* should do just that. Professor Simon has drawn from a long and profound study of the relations between Christianity and Judaism, and has produced a work both of synthesis and of originality. It should make a valuable contribution to scholarly discussion while at the same time providing the general reader with a useful introduction to the subject.

Certain technical matters call for a few words of comment. The primary goal of the translator, apart from the actual work of translation, has been to provide the English reader with as useful a book as possible. To this end, certain additions and clarifications have been made in the technical apparatus of the book. Specifically, the bibliography has been enlarged substantially and updated by the addition of works in English, including translations of works listed in the original bibliography where such translations have been known to exist; a glossary of unfamiliar terms has been appended; and an index has been provided. Occasionally, translator's footnotes have been added to clarify certain items in the text or to give further references to works in English; these footnotes have been enclosed in brackets.

In regard to the spelling of unfamiliar names, it must be added that a rule of thumb has been used. After consulting several scholarly sources for any given name, the consensus has been followed. Often no such consensus exists. In such cases, the aim has been to make the name recognizable to the reader.

The same rule of thumb has been followed for the transliteration of Hebrew words, the procedures for which are at present somewhat in flux (the principles for the transliteration of Greek are fairly standard). The spelling of Hebrew words has been normalized by omitting diacritical marks.

Titles of classical Greek and Latin authors have been given in English. For standard Latin titles, see the list of abbreviations.

Quotations from the writings of Philo, Josephus, and Pliny are taken from the Loeb Classical Library and are used with the permission of Harvard University Press. Passages from Book Two of *The Jewish War* are cited in the translation of Dupont-Sommer, *The Essene Writings*, pp. 26-36, and are used with permission of the publishers, Basil Blackwell and World Publishing Company. Unless otherwise specified, biblical quotations are from the Revised Standard Version.

I would like to take this opportunity to express my

appreciation to Professor Simon for his hospitality to me during my period of study at Strasbourg in 1962-64.

My gratitude is due also my sister, Mrs. Charles W. Young, whose unerring skill in catching and correcting infelicitous words and phrases has been invaluable, and who typed the manuscript in final form. The present translation owes much to her dedicated and poorly rewarded labors.

Those infelicities and obscure renderings which remain in the translation are, of course, my own responsibility.

Douglass College   JAMES H. FARLEY
New Brunswick, New Jersey
June, 1966

Foreword

THIS BRIEF BOOK should have been written
by Roger Goossens, late professor of the Free University of Brussels. His death came before he was able to
complete the task. From his abundant but incom-
pletely organized notes, and from chapters that were
partially edited but unpublishable as they stood, I
have tried to utilize as much as possible. I am not
certain that I have been fully successful in this
attempt. It is always a delicate task to continue a work
begun by another. In doing so, one courts the twofold
risk of distorting the thought of one's predecessor and
of betraying one's own thought. But, in fact, I have
not had too much difficulty following the course laid
out by Goossens. This is not to say that there are no
divergences from his project at certain points. Such
divergences are numerous and important enough to
make this brief essay appreciably different, both in
total scope and in details, from that which Goossens
himself would have presented to his readers. Yet,
even though I have been able neither to reproduce
word for word the manuscript fragments entrusted to
me, nor to fill in the gaps exactly as he would have

done, I have tried to remain faithful to the spirit that animated his research. And I would like my modest work to be a tribute to the memory of this scholar, lamented by so many.

The truly remarkable discovery of the Dead Sea scrolls posed the temptation of limiting this study to those documents. I have felt it necessary to resist this temptation. The Qumran community, suddenly thrown into the spotlight of scholarly interest, assuredly seems to be one of the most important of the Jewish sects, its importance lying more in the influence that radiated from it than in its numerical strength. And today it is the group with which we are best acquainted. Yet this is not sufficient reason to neglect all the other groups. There is already an enormous literature on the Essenes, and it is not my desire to add another book to the list. Rather, I have thought it of more value to consider the Essenes in their proper perspective by seeing them within the framework of a necessarily summary and superficial over-all picture of the various currents that, sometimes running parallel, sometimes intermingling, and sometimes colliding, constituted Judaism in the time of Christ.

Contents

Contents—continued

ABBREVIATIONS

I. AUTHORS

EUSEBIUS OF CAESAREA

Eccl. Hist.	*Ecclesiastical History (Historia Ecclesiastica)*
Praep. Ev.	*Praeparatio Evangelica*

FLAVIUS JOSEPHUS

Ant.	*Antiquities of the Jews (Antiquitates Iudaeorum)*
Life	*Life of Flavius Josephus (Vita)*
War	*The Jewish War (Bellum Iudaicum)*

JUSTIN MARTYR

Dialogue	*Dialogue with Trypho*

PHILO OF ALEXANDRIA

Apology	*Apology for the Jews (Apologia pro Iudaeis; Loeb: Hypothetica)*
Con. Tongues	*On the Confusion of Tongues (De Confusione Linguarum)*
Cont. Life	*On the Contemplative Life (De Vita Contemplativa)*
Every Good Man	*Every Good Man Is Free (Quod Omnis Probus Liber Sit)*
Heir	*Who Is the Heir of Divine Things (Quis Rerum Divinarum Heres)*
Mig. Abr.	*On the Migration of Abraham (De Migratione Abrahami)*
On the Creation	*On the Account of the World's Creation Given by Moses (De Opificio Mundi)*

PLINY THE ELDER

Nat. Hist.	*Natural History (Naturalis Historia)*

II. OTHER ABBREVIATIONS

JBL	*Journal of Biblical Literature*
NEB	*The New English Bible: New Testament* (Oxford and Cambridge University Presses, 1961)
NT	*Novum Testamentum*
NTS	*New Testament Studies*
RB	*Revue biblique*
RHPR	*Revue d'Histoire et de Philosophie religieuses*

1

Definition and
Characteristics of
the Jewish Sects

IN CONTRAST to Christianity, with its many branches, Judaism is all too often thought of as an integral bloc, a monolithic religion. Yet even with respect to contemporary Judaism, this view is too schematic and approximate. Samaritans and Karaites still exist in the Near East, even though they are few in number. Both groups are dissentient Jews and, from the point of view of synagogue orthodoxy, heretics. Occidental Judaism, for its part, is far from presenting an absolute unity and cohesiveness. For example, American Judaism, by far the most important numerically, comprises three clearly distinct currents. Although Orthodox, Conservative, and Reform (Liberal) Jews maintain cordial relationships with one another, they are nonetheless organized into autonomous groupings, which are neither more nor less interdependent than are the various churches issuing from the Reformation. In their various ways,

1

these three branches of Judaism at least are connected to the common trunk of Pharisaism through the rabbinical tradition of the Middle Ages and the Talmud. But at the beginning of the Christian era, Pharisaism itself represented only one of the major streams in the midst of a Judaism obviously even more variegated than it is today.

Anyone who has read the Gospels is acquainted with the name of the Pharisees, as well as that of their rivals, the Sadducees. The first-century Jewish historian Flavius Josephus is our primary source in this matter. Besides the Pharisees and the Sadducees, he names and describes two other groups, the Essenes and the Zealots. The picture that he paints is primarily of Palestine. But even during this period the majority of the Jews lived outside the Holy Land, in the diaspora, or dispersion. The diaspora came into being at the time of the Babylonian exile. From the time of Alexander the Great onward, it was enlarged by an uninterrupted movement of emigration from Palestine, sometimes spontaneous, sometimes forced.

Having been thus placed in permanent contact with the Hellenistic (later Greco-Roman) world, the Jews came under its influence to varying degrees. In certain circles, the influence was profound enough to weaken the structures of the observance of the law and even, sometimes, the observance of monotheism. We catch glimpses of groups on the fringes of Judaism and paganism that drew inspiration from both Judaism and paganism, groups whose adherents no doubt came from both sides. These extremist groups are undoubtedly too far along on the road to syncretism and compromise to be considered as authentic representatives of Jewish religious life. It is certain that there were external influences— Semitic, Egyptian, Greek, or Persian—exerting themselves more or less strongly both in Palestine and in the diaspora. Even if we ignore the previously mentioned fringe groups, these external influences were an important element in bringing about the many and diverse factions within a religion whose unity, on first sight, impressed the foreign observer, just as it does today.

To be sure, this is a real unity, but it is hardly uniformity. Far from it. We have already referred to the groups mentioned by Josephus. Philo of Alexandria, a contemporary of Christ, has left us with a description of another group called the Therapeutae. Also influential at the time was the philosophical Judaism of certain Alexandrian circles, of which Philo himself was the most characteristic representative. Add to these the groups whose names have been preserved for us by certain ecclesiastical writers of antiquity and we get an idea, undoubtedly still incomplete, of the variety of movements and schools present in the Judaism of Jesus' age. It is convenient, in this connection, to speak of sects. But in order to avoid any possible misunderstandings, it is necessary to state precisely what is meant by the term "sect."

As the term is most commonly used today, it belongs to the vocabulary of Christianity. And even there it is not used with perfect ease and assurance. In fact, in recent years it has given rise to some interesting discussions. Moreover, it is difficult to define "sect" in a way that is entirely satisfactory and, especially, universally accepted. "To the Catholic," we are told, "the distinction of church and sect presents no difficulty. For him any Christian denomination which has set itself up independently of his own church is a sect."[1] Such is the theory. But in fact, not many knowledgeable Catholics can be found who are ready to label as sects the great denominations that issued from the Reformation—Lutheran, Reformed, or Anglican. In any case, it is evident that none of the many varieties of Christianity is disposed to apply this label to itself. For the term bears a certain pejorative connotation, undoubtedly more subtle than in the epithet "sectarian," but clear enough nonetheless to make one hesitant about proclaiming oneself an adherent of a sect. The term "church" has a different connotation and a different allure.

If we were to try to strip this unfortunate connotation from the word "sect" to make it a simple technical term without emotional implication, we would be tempted to apply it to the numerically weak religious groups of exclusivistic spirit, to those small armies of the elect that are in opposition to the great, multitudinous church. In this manner we would see a quantitative difference between church and sect. But in such an approach it is sometimes difficult to say where

---

[1] "Sect and Sects," *The Catholic Encyclopedia*, vol. 13. (New York: Appleton, 1912), p. 675.

the line of demarcation lies. In France, the Baptists, in their essentially Roman Catholic context, would seem to be a sect. In the United States, where their twenty-three million members make them the strongest of the Protestant groups, it is impossible to deny them the designation "church" if the criterion of numbers is employed. Indeed, the numerical factor is not the only one to take into account; it is not even the most important: a given group, which has begun with the modest dimensions of a sect, can later develop the dimensions of a church. Even more than the number of its members, it is its nature as a separated group that defines the sect for the historian of Christianity. The rupture can be caused by a formal excommunication, or it can come on the sect's own initiative. In both cases, the sect is characterized by opposition to a norm commonly accepted in the church from which it has issued; a conciliar or pontifical decision, an ecclesiastical tradition, or a confession of faith can be the original stumbling block.

Actually, the term "sect" tends to be used especially, although not exclusively, for those groups that formed on the fringes of the churches founded by the great Reformers of the sixteenth century or standing in the tradition of their teachings. Such sects carry the principle of individual interpretation of Scripture further than the Reformers did; thus they represent a victory of religious individualism over ecclesiastical institutions. In relation to Roman Catholicism, these sects constitute something like a twice-removed schism. In this sense, one would be justified in speaking of the Seventh-day Adventist sect, or the sect of the Jehovah's Witnesses.

Christian perspectives, then, are relatively clear in this respect. Jewish perspectives are less clear, and totally different. First of all, Judaism at the time of Christ had no universally recognized magisterium capable of formulating the norms of the faith. The duties of the priesthood lay in the area of ritual. The Sanhedrin was a court of justice whose function was to interpret and apply the law of Moses, rather than a council occupied with formulating doctrinal statements. Moreover, the Sanhedrin was far from representing a homogeneous point of view. The rabbis, who during this period increasingly assumed the role of spiritual leaders of the Chosen People, also devoted themselves to the interpretation of the Torah's stipulations. Their interpretations were made in the light of a tradition transmitted from generation to generation, although among the various schools there were considerable variations and even contradictions.

Beyond their differences of opinion, the priesthood, the Sanhedrin, and the rabbinical schools at least had in common that they were preoccupied with practice and conduct more than with doctrine: observance was at the center of their thought and discussion.

Indeed, the paucity of the doctrinal content of Judaism, along with the absence of a universally accepted authority in the matter, helps to explain the rather indefinite nature of its idea of orthodoxy. To be a Jew was essentially to comply with the moral and ritual imperatives of the Torah, the charter of the covenant with the one God, whose will the Torah records. And the monotheistic affirmation, the *shema*, was the only confession of faith known in Judaism at the beginning of our era: "Hear, O Israel: The Lord our God is one Lord" (Deut. 6:4). This monotheistic affirmation was not to become precise and explicit until Maimonides and his Thirteen Principles. Even these Principles, although they figure in the liturgy of the synagogue, have an authority that is more traditional than properly normative. And in the twentieth century, Judaism remains above all an orthodoxy of practice rather than of doctrine.

Under these conditions, it is understandable that, at the beginning of the Christian era, no absolutely strict line of demarcation could be drawn between orthodoxy and heterodoxy. The Jewish sects, then, were not radically aberrant groups vis-à-vis the official synagogue. Nor were they separated from each other in the way that the two hundred and fifty or so Christian "sects" of the United States are today. They were, rather, various currents that, taken together, constituted Judaism. Moreover, each one could claim, with some semblance of justification, to represent the most authentic form of Judaism.

Only the Samaritans were at this time clearly distinct from the Jewish community: they are a sect in the modern usage of the term. Israel rejected them with abhorrence, and refused to consider them as Jews. There were several reasons for this attitude toward the Samaritans. For one thing, the Samaritans accepted the Pentateuch alone as inspired Scripture. Also, refusing to admit the temple in Jerusalem as the authentic dwelling place of God, they offered their sacrifices on Mount Gerizim. Furthermore, in all likelihood, their religion, although hardened into somewhat archaic forms, was strongly syncretistic. But the primary cause of this hostility between Samaritans and Jews can be traced to the political schism that split Solomon's kingdom in two. This dissidence was perpetuated on another plane after the end of Jewish national independence. Other groups in Israel had been permitted to profess views that were similar enough, in certain respects, to those of the Samaritans without being excommunicated for doing so. The reason is simply that these groups were formed after the separation of the two kingdoms or at the onset of foreign domination. Furthermore, circumstances reinforced, or at least maintained, the solidarity of these groups vis-à-vis a religion that was also a people, as it was in the case of the Jews.

Two elements coexisted in the Sanhedrin itself, two largely antagonistic "sects," the Pharisees and the Sadducees. Both worshiped the same God, but their agreement did not go much further than that. On all other points their opposition was complete. Both groups had been brought to a privileged position through the force of circumstance, and, at the price of a *modus vivendi* that muted their quarrels, they were able to maintain this position. Yet this does not authorize us to view them as the only qualified representatives of true Judaism, in opposition to "heretics" on all sides. It is significant that Josephus employs the term *hairesis* to designate the Pharisees and the Sadducees as well as the Essenes. Josephus' use of the term is a convenient reminder to those who would consider the Essenes as "heretics" (in the modern sense of the word) that the structures of Judaism are not those of Christianity. The Greek term from which we have derived the word "heresy" means simply a religious or philosophic choice, an option. It implies neither the idea of differentiation and separation with respect to a norm considered as the only one valid, nor, *a fortiori*, the pejorative connotation that attaches to the English word.

In the final analysis, it is both convenient and legitimate to speak of Jewish sects, on the condition that we include nothing more in the meaning of the term than the Latins did when they translated *hairesis* as *secta*. The Pharisees were a sect, the Sadducees were a sect, just as were the Essenes. Josephus, who studied these movements side by side, saw in them three equally valid forms of Judaism. We will not erect barriers where he refused to see any.

Nevertheless, in the eyes of the modern historian a dividing line does exist. This line does not separate and place in opposition orthodoxy and heresy properly so-called, but rather official Judaism (that of the Sanhedrin and of Jerusalem), on the one hand, and what could be called peripheral or marginal Judaism, on the other hand. This latter was undoubtedly composed of a considerable number of other sects, among which the Essenes stand out in particularly bold relief. This is not a rigid dividing line. It is affected by various fluctuations, so that a given group will appear sometimes on one side, sometimes on the other.

For example, at the beginning of their history the Pharisees were a handful of dissidents, sectarians in the most precise meaning of the term. Indeed, their very name means "separated," those who constitute a group apart. But in the period with which we are concerned, the situation was completely reversed: not only had the Pharisees become the most powerful religious party, they were also the spiritual leaders most widely heeded by the people. Their criteria were, increasingly, the ones that defined the good Jew.

In spite of the divergent currents, official Judaism, under the direction of the Pharisees, tended to evolve in the direction of an orthodoxy. The final fixing of this orthodoxy was hindered by the existence of the Sadducean party, and would not be triumphant until seventy years later, in Talmudic rabbinism.

Forms of Deviation

Three forms of "sectarian" deviation were possible over against the increasingly influential Pharisaic norms—ritual, scriptural, doctrinal. As we shall see, the Pharisees themselves had set the example for such deviation. In reaction to the hardened positions of Sadducean conservatism, the Pharisees had made various liturgical, scriptural, and doctrinal innovations. From then on, it became increasingly the case that anyone who deviated one way or the other from the Pharisaic position was suspect of heresy (in the modern sense).

On the level of ritual, excessive zeal in observance was, in certain cases, viewed as unfavorably as indifference. And Pharisaic casuistry endeavored to fix the limits within which Jewish religious practice could legitimately operate.

On the scriptural plane, deviation could consist either in a reduction and purging of the canon of the synagogue, or in an enlarging of it. The Samaritans were heretics, distinctly cut off from the Jewish community, because they restricted their canon to the Pentateuch. But in the eyes of the Pharisees, the Sadducees were also heretics for holding to the letter of the written text and rejecting all the additions and interpretations of oral tradition. The Samaritans and Sadducees represented, to varying degrees, what could be called the reactionary right. But we also catch glimpses of a progressivist left which, alongside the books of the official canon, revered and utilized other texts considered equally inspired. These texts were more or less esoteric in nature (the Dead Sea scrolls have given us a great deal of information concerning the library of the large Essenian confraternity).

In the area of doctrine, finally, monotheism was the touchstone. Or better, monotheism *was* Judaism. But the concept was open to various interpretations and,

indeed, was rather pliable. It was more or less susceptible to the influences of Greek philosophic speculation, and more or less receptive to the lures of dualism. It is possible to conceive the relationship between Creator and creation in various ways, to propose different solutions to the problem of evil: gnosticism has certain roots in Jewish speculation, and in
turn influenced the further development of Jewish
speculation. Rabbinic legalism, not matter how strong
and imposing it was, still did not exclude a more
mystical type of religiosity. The first features of what
later became the Kabbalah began to emerge. Scattered among the people were the ferments of a rather
anarchical individualism regarding the official norms.
The place of the temple in Jewish religion was not
accepted everywhere without reservations: here and
there we see attitudes of defiance and even of rejection of the sanctuary and its ritual. A number of
questions were raised, concerning which the Bible
said little or nothing. Yet the pious mentality required
answers. Problems relating to eschatology, messianism, and the future life were passionately scrutinized
and debated, and brought forth a multitude of contradictory solutions.

Ritualistic, scriptural, and doctrinal deviations
came together in multifarious combinations, defining
a whole gamut of movements and groupings that we
too often assume to be of secondary importance in
Jewish religious life. Sometimes these deviations were
coupled together. At other times, as it appears to us,
they operated in inverse directions. Thus doctrinal

laxity and laxity of observance did not always necessarily go in pairs. It was sometimes the case that an inflexible legalistic rigorism, fixing a rigid orthodoxy of practice, was accompanied by an attitude toward beliefs that was strongly receptive to outside influences (witness, for example, Philo of Alexandria). The Pharisees themselves, so preoccupied with erecting the barrier of observances around the Chosen People in order to isolate them from the impure *goyim*, were able, under the cover of this barrier, to enrich certain aspects of their teaching with elements borrowed from the Persian and Greek worlds. The case of the Essenes is equally clear. These rigorists of observance, fanatics compared to average Judaism, were also open (as the Dead Sea scrolls attest) to a number of outside speculations that were foreign to the ancient foundations of Israelite and biblical thought.

Everything was still in a state of flux in this infinitely complex phenomenon that was Judaism around the beginning of the Christian era. To be sure, the party of the Pharisees already held the key positions and tended to impose their norms. However, its supremacy was not yet uncontested. Nor were the excommunications it attempted to pronounce any more decisive: they ran headlong into counter excommunications, for example, those which the Essene community at Qumran formulated against the whole mass of Israelites, Pharisees included.

With the Essenes we encounter what would seem to be a sect, with its self-imposed segregation and its

13

fanatical exclusivism. And yet Josephus, who admired the Essenes, could not bring himself to cut off from Judaism one of its hardiest branches.

In short, all was in flux, dependent both on political vicissitudes and local conditions. The Hasmonean period was dominated by the conflict between Sadducees and Pharisees, who took turns contending for and exercising ascendancy (according to the personal dispositions of the successive sovereigns). At the beginning of the Christian era a rather shaky balance existed, a balance already tending to weigh in favor of the Pharisees.

The history of the Qumran community, insofar as we can reconstruct it, reflects even more clearly the influence, often determining, of the circumstances of the hour. Periods of tension, and even of persecution and flight from Palestine, alternated with periods of peaceful calm and fruitful progress. On the eve of the crisis of A.D. 70, the parties in power (the Pharisees and the Sadducees) continue to regard the Qumran community with mistrust. This mistrust was greater on the part of the Sadducees, who nourished only antipathy toward Qumran. But it is not impossible that the reactions of the Pharisees were tempered with a discreet admiration for these eccentrics who were, after all, giants of observance.

In any case, the inhospitable banks of the Dead Sea assured the Qumran community an almost complete impunity. Many things were possible in the depths of the desert, or even in the remote corners of the diaspora, which, if proclaimed in the squares of Jerusalem, would not fail to elicit hostile reactions from the religious and political authorities. There were undoubtedly a considerable number of conventicles that developed in this way on the periphery of Israel. Perhaps some of them passed into complete and final schism. But more often they retained some tie, no matter how loose, with the trunk from which they had sprung. Thus a study of Jewish sects around the beginning of the Christian era must be within the framework of official Judaism vis-à-vis marginal Judaism.

But we must not forget that the total number of Jewish sects represented only a tiny minority in relation to the global population of the Jewish faithful. It is likely that the total population of Palestine at the time of Christ was about five-hundred thousand. Josephus gives a figure of six thousand for the Pharisees, and four thousand for the Essenes; he does not indicate the number of Sadducees, but comments that they were not very numerous. In other words, although the great majority of Jews could not escape the influence of the sects, they were still located outside the ranks of the sects. For the most part, the majority belonged to the *amme ha arez* ("people of the land"), a rabbinical expression designating the common people, the man in the street.

The religion of this undifferentiated mass presented no distinctive characteristics, although it was appreciably less demanding and undoubtedly more lukewarm than that of the organized religious parties.

Thus we find some Jewish sects installed in official

positions, with the reins of power in hand, and others, on the contrary, confined to the periphery. But they all had one thing in common: their aloofness was not in relation to an ecclesiastical norm, but in relation to the masses. Of course, over against the pagan troops that occupied the land, this aversion was tempered by a relative solidarity with every Israelite, no matter how odious he might be. The Roman presence was a unitive factor. But this presence did not quite succeed in smothering the aristocratic haughtiness of the Sadducees or the pride of the scholarly and puritanical Pharisee doctor of the law. Especially, it was not able to stifle the proud conviction among the Essenes and other marginal conventicles that their particular group constituted the "small remnant" of the only elect. In Jewish sectarian life we shall encounter once again two of the customary features of every sect: smallness of numbers and an acute feeling of difference and superiority, an acute consciousness of election.

2

Sadducees, Pharisees, and Zealots

A PRECISE DATE cannot be assigned to the birth of Jewish sectarian life as a whole, nor to that of its various component groups. However far one traces back the religious history of Israel, there are always found both a tendency toward unification and elements that resisted and avoided unification.

The first attempt at unification clearly came with the construction of the temple, with the concentration of the cult at Jerusalem in the hands of an official priesthood, and in the various stages of the codification of the law. But centrifugal forces always remained active. The old local sanctuaries continued for a long time to exert their attraction, just as had the forms of religious life that existed in Canaan before the Hebrew's arrival (or, inversely, just as had the forms of religious life practiced by the Hebrews before they settled in Palestine). Some people were not at all satisfied with the type of religion that had been developed at Jerusalem by the monarchy and the priests. Some found it too far removed from the ancient Hebrew tradition, too much contaminated by autochthonous cultic practices; others would have liked to have given an even larger place to these cultic practices. There are suggestions of syncretistic rites taking place at the sanctuaries of the countryside, and this situation undoubtedly brought about a considerable modification of the strictness of Yahwist monotheism. At the other extreme were the Rechabites. This group existed in Palestine several centuries after it had been first settled by the Hebrews. Yet even at that late date they refused to sow seed, to drink wine, or to build houses (Jer. 35:6-10). This attitude expressed a nostalgia for the desert and for the nomadic life, and a protest against all aspects of sedentary culture. However, the Rechabites were only the prefiguration of a sect. The same is true of the Nazirites (Num., chap. 6), pious ascetics whose vows, moreover, were only temporary.

Indeed, the appearance of sects—that is to say, of quite distinct groups that differed from one another on important points of belief or practice—resulted from the establishing of closer contacts between Israel and the surrounding civilizations. Their appearance was linked to the various reactions of the Jews to cultural and religious influences from the outside. In this regard, the exile was of fundamental importance, and the setting up of Hellenistic monarchies even more so. As far as we can tell from available documents, Israel first became seriously divided on basic questions in the second century B.C., on contact with the Seleucid dynasty.

Certain Jews, impressed by the splendor of Hellenistic civilization, began to observe "the ordinances of the Gentiles" at Jerusalem. They "removed the marks of circumcision, and abandoned the holy covenant" (1 Macc. 1:15-16). When Antiochus Epiphanes, king of Syria (175-164 B.C.), having become master of the city, pillaged and profaned the temple and introduced there "the abomination of desolation" (i.e., a pagan altar or a statue of a god), some of the Jews sacrificed to the idols. Others, however, defying persecution, organized an armed resistance in the name of the religion of their fathers. The signal for revolt was given at Modein by Mattathias and his sons, from whom came the priestly dynasty commonly known as the Maccabees or the Hasmoneans. This handful of insurgents was joined by a troop of Hasideans (*hasidim*). We are justified in recognizing these "mighty warriors of Israel, every one who offered himself willingly for the law" (1 Macc. 2:42), as the first Jewish "sect." This group was characterized by religious as well as patriotic intransigence, as compared to the accommodating laxity of the masses who, having made concessions to Greek culture, went on to do the same regarding paganism, and sometimes went as far as outright apostasy. Some authors see in this group the point of departure of the Pharisaic movement; others see in it the first rough outlines of Essenism. It is quite possible that the *hasidim* were the common ancestors of both sects, each of which was characterized by a legalistic zeal. And it is undoubtedly in this same period, in connection with these same events, that we must look for the origins and the first outlines of the religious tripartition described by Josephus. Indeed, it is in this same context that he first mentions this tripartite cleavage.

If we are indeed able to identify the Essenes with the sect of Qumran revealed to us by the Dead Sea scrolls (and everything indicates that we may), then it is clear that they were in opposition to the official Judaism of the capital both on matters of observance and belief, and also because they did not recognize the Jerusalem priesthood as legitimate. In calling themselves "sons of Zadok" (this is, in all probability, descendants of the high priest installed by Solomon, 1 Kings 2:35), the Qumran sectarians claimed the quality of legitimate priests, in opposition to the usurpers of the temple. These latter were, from the beginning, none other than the Hasmoneans, obscure village priests who after their victory were promoted to the ruling (and hereditary) high priesthood which was later associated with the monarchy.

Thus the nucleus of the Essenian sect would be composed of members of old priestly families, supporters of the Maccabees at the time of the insurrection but who were later ranged against them in an uncompromising rivalry. Of course, the ranks of the *hasidim* were not composed solely of priests. In fact, it is more likely that the priests were in the minority among a much larger number of pious laymen. These laymen could well have constituted the initial framework of Pharisaism, which, as we shall see, never seemed to have particularly close attachments with the clergy. Indeed, since these laymen were less sensitive than the priests to questions of sacerdotal legitimacy, they could remain faithful to the first Hasmoneans after the Maccabean revolt had ended in victory.

According to Josephus, it was not until the reign of John Hyrcanus (135-104 B.C.) that the split came between the high priesthood and the Pharisees. Perhaps it came even later, under the reign of Alexander Jannaeus (103-76 B.C.). Whatever date we adopt (and we need not discuss it here), it is almost certain that the break came later than the secession of the sons of Zadok, the ancestors of the Essenes of Qumran. Josephus states that the break was motivated by the fact that a Pharisee named Eleazar asked Hyrcanus to renounce his religious authority and keep only his civil power. This explanation is not unlikely. Indeed, a significant number of Jews felt that the separation of the spiritual and the temporal, of the priesthood and the monarchy, was an intangible principle, fixed from the time of David. The concentration of all the powers in the hands of one person, together with the overly autocratic tendencies of the Hasmoneans, must have been an intolerable abuse for the Pharisees, for political as well as religious reasons. Moreover, these puritans undoubtedly reproached the dynasty, or certain of its representatives, for having disappointed their hopes of a restoration of hasidic rule and for making excessive concessions, in turn, to Hellenism and the foreigner whom they had formerly opposed.

The official favor from which the Pharisees had benefited in the beginning now passed to the Sadducees. It was not until toward the end of the Hasmonean period that the Pharisees returned to favor and regained momentarily their determining influence. But the rivalry of the two parties was thenceforth, and up to the destruction of the temple in A.D. 70, one of the dominant features of Jewish religious history. This rivalry was acute and sometimes violent under the last Hasmoneans. Although it never disappeared entirely, it became less acute once Roman domination was set up in Palestine (63 B.C.) and after the vassal dynasty of Herod the Great had been established.

Sadducees

Josephus is our primary source of information on the three major groups or sects.[1] The picture he paints is certainly oversimplified and oversystematized. In particular, we must not take literally the correlation he makes between Sadducees and Epicureans, between Pharisees and Stoics or, as we shall see later, between Essenes and Pythagoreans. Such correlation was an attempt to help the Gentiles understand the religious realities of Judaism, and is only partially true. All we have available as complement and corrective to Josephus are a few sparse items of information from the New Testament and from Jewish and

---

[1] The relevant passages in Josephus are *Ant.* 13.5.9, 13.10.6, 18.1.2 ff.; *War* 2.8.14; *Life* 28.

Christian writings of the following centuries. The New Testament material is of little assistance, since it is both slight and of somewhat questionable objectivity. The evangelists were sympathetic neither to the Pharisees nor to the Sadducees, and were especially keen on pointing out their faults. The same point of view reappears, somewhat modified, in the writings of later ecclesiastical authors.

On the other hand, since the rabbinical writings came from the very circles where the spirit of Pharisaism survived after A.D. 70, we can reconstruct a fairly faithful picture of that sect. But the same cannot be said for the Sadducees. We possess no document that can be attributed to them with certainty. Furthermore, whereas the first Christians rightly considered the Sadducees to be their present and immediate enemies, the rabbis of the Talmud, for their part, knew the Sadducees only through tradition. It cannot be said that the rabbis felt any great affection for them. It is very difficult, under these conditions, to form any exact and impartial idea of the Sadducees.

The etymology of their name (Greek *Saddoukaioi*, Hebrew *Zaddukim*) is much disputed. It is quite possible that it should be linked, along with the *bene Zadok* ("sons of Zadok") of Qumran, to the high priest at the time of Solomon. It should not be surprising that two rival groups, one of which seems to have persecuted the other from time to time, both claimed the same historical personage: in laying claim to this spiritual lineage, each group affirmed its pretension to being the legitimate priesthood, in accordance with the principle proclaimed by Ezekiel: "These are the sons of Zadok, who alone among the sons of Levi may come near to the Lord to minister to him" (Ezek. 40:46).

The Sadducees indeed came mostly from the priestly class, although the two groups were never identical. They represented an aristocracy that seems to have been haughty and exclusive. They had little contact with the people and little influence over them. At the beginning of the Christian era their authority, primarily cultic, seems scarcely to have gone beyond the confines of the temple. Even in the Sanhedrin they were obliged to accept the presence and often, undoubtedly, the preponderance of the Pharisees. When the temple was destroyed, they disappeared with it. Even before A.D. 70, the center of gravity of the religious life had shifted from the single sanctuary to the synagogues, scattered everywhere throughout Palestine and the diaspora. For the most part, the synagogues gave expression to the Pharisaic ideal.

In every respect, the Sadducees represented the past. They were conservatives in politics as well as in religion. With respect to the upsurge of messianic expectation the Sadducees manifested the hostility of the powers that be against any movement tending to subvert the established order. In this case, it was the Roman order. But this order guaranteed their own interests, and the Sadducees were in complete solidarity with the occupiers, since the Romans permitted them to practice their religion freely.

This religion was governed by the law, as it was codified in the Bible: the Sadducees "hold that only those regulations should be considered valid which were written down (in Scripture), and that those which had been handed down by former generations need not be observed" (*Ant.* 13.10.6). According to certain Christian writers of antiquity, the Sadducees, like the Samaritans, recognized only the Pentateuch as canonical, the Mosaic Torah in the narrow sense. This view is undoubtedly erroneous. To be sure, it is not difficult to imagine that the Sadducees held the writings of the prophets in low esteem, for the message of the prophets was not designed to please those upon whom fortune had smiled. But it is doubtful that this antipathy was pushed to the point of excluding the prophetic writings from the official canon of Scripture. As the Septuagint attests, the canon was already fixed in much the same form as we know it.

What is certain, however, is that the Sadducees were opposed to any ritual or doctrinal innovation: it was on this point that they were in fundamental opposition to the Pharisees. This attitude led them, as far as observance was concerned, to an oscillation between attenuating the rigorism of the Pharisees and accentuating it. Such oscillation was a necessary reaction to the refined casuistry of the rabbis. This casuistry sometimes ended with the rabbis going the strictness of the written commandments one better; but it could also produce something of a stretching of the written commandments. The Sadducees, on the contrary, did not indulge in biblical interpretation. They held strictly to the letter of the law. For this reason there were far fewer nuances in their position. For example, Josephus says that the Sadducees were quite severe in meting out justice. Such a trait should not surprise us in these upholders of the established order. It would certainly not do them an injustice to suspect them of a certain amount of conformity.

This fundamental conservatism also explains their doctrinal peculiarities. According to Josephus, they denied the sovereignty of fate and even the intervention of God in the world and in the affairs of men. Man, in the view of the Sadducees, has unrestricted free will. They did not believe in the continued existence of the soul after death; on the contrary, they believed that it died with the body and, consequently, they denied "penalties in the underworld, and rewards" (*War* 2.8.14). It is likely that Josephus, in attempting to be understood, overhellenized the Sadducees. It is difficult to believe that any section of Judaism was able to relegate God to the position of impassive inaction that certain Greek thinkers attributed to him, thus denying providence; for it is providence that is implied when Josephus speaks of fate (*heimarmenē*), an idea that was not very Jewish. It is not impossible, of course, that the Sadducees held the views on the afterlife that are attributed to them. However, the New Testament is perhaps closer to the truth when it says that the Sadducees denied resurrection (Matt. 22:23; Acts 23:8). For the most part, the Jews had difficulty conceiving of a completely disembodied soul; for them, in general, resurrection was the very condition of immortality. Since all but the latest parts of the Old Testament say very little about life after death, it was quite consistent for the Sadducees, remaining true to their fundamental principle of fidelity to the written text, to forbid any precise formulations. Without going to the extreme of categorically denying survival after death, they could maintain a prudent agnosticism in this respect. Thus we can imagine that the Sadducees, satisfied with their lot here below, were not disposed to scrutinize the mysteries of the beyond.

The New Testament also tells us that the Sadducees did not believe in angels or spirits (Acts 23:8). Evil spirits and demons are undoubtedly meant. Perhaps this too is an oversimplification. Angels are frequently mentioned in the Bible and even in the Pentateuch. What is probably implied in this passage from Acts is that the Sadducees repudiated the frequency magical and astrological speculations of certain sectors of Judaism, speculations that promoted, in particular, the very highly developed angelology of the Pharisees. In this, as in all other matters, their attitude expressed the ritualist's indifference (or at least relative indifference) to all doctrinal elaborations, as well as the conservative's hostility to all innovation.

Pharisees

The name of the Pharisees, according to the most widely accepted etymology, means "the separated ones" (from the Hebrew root *parash*). This is an allusion to the origins of the movement, which came into being as a sect of rigorists, set apart from the masses. Another etymology has been proposed by T. W. Manson. Manson holds that the term "originally meant simply 'Persian' " (the Hebrew form of both words is indeed almost the same).[2] In this view, the term would be a pejorative nickname applied by their enemies to men whose belief, in many respects, obviously reflected the influence of Persian concepts. Manson's view has not found many supporters. Yet it is necessary to mention it here, for it emphasizes the major characteristics of the Pharisee sect: on the matter of observances they maintained a punctilious legalism, while in doctrinal matters they had a quite open and receptive spirit.

Josephus' observations concerning the Pharisees are relatively precise. But he does not say a great deal about them, and what he does say is often vitiated by a certain embellishment. We are fortunate in having other sources of information regarding the Pharisees, namely, the Gospels and the rabbinical writings. Of course, the picture drawn by the evangelists is hardly flattering. For the most part it expresses the animosity of the first Christians to their most formidable adversaries. Jewish religious opposition, in fact, was organized around Pharisaism, and it was on this that the preaching of the nascent church in Israel finally shattered. Rabbinical literature, and especially the

---

[2] T. W. Manson, *The Servant Messiah* (Cambridge University Press, 1953), p. 19.

Talmud, is of invaluable help to us in this matter. For one thing, it furnishes a partial confirmation of the Gospel accounts. But at the same time it provides the necessary complements and corrections. Through the rabbinical literature we come to the heart of Pharisaic thought itself. Indeed, there is no doubt that these documents, all written later than the period which concerns us, faithfully perpetuated the methods and the spirit of the sect. These documents do not bear the name "Pharisee," because the sect had ceased to exist as such. The events of A.D. 70 definitively removed the Sadducees from the scene. The other sects had disappeared, having died or been absorbed either into the church or into the Pharisaic synagogue itself. Thus the Pharisees remained practically alone, until new schisms would arise. They no longer had any reason, therefore, to call themselves Pharisees, since this title denoted being set apart. There no longer existed any group from which to be set apart. They were quite simply Jews, or rather, they were *the* Jews. Pharisaism and Judaism were now coextensive.

In the Gospel of Matthew we find a vehement diatribe placed in the mouth of Jesus by the evangelist (23:1-36), which repeats over and over the formula, "Woe unto you, scribes and Pharisees, hypocrites!" Ordinary speech, supported by the Matthean passage, has turned the term "Pharisee" into a synonym for the epithet placed alongside it in these verses. Even among scholars, the Pharisees have long had a bad reputation. But a salutary reaction has set in among recent generations of scholars, Christian as well as Jewish. Today we realize that the picture drawn by the Gospel writers, sometimes exaggerated to the point of caricature, has retained only the most questionable traits and the most conspicuous faults of the sect. The picture is not completely false, in the sense that there were undoubtedly hypocrites and those who pretended to be religious among the Pharisees. But it is a partial and prejudiced picture. Surely it would be as unjust to seek the authentic image of the Pharisee in this picture as it would be to present Tartuffe as the exact portrait of the Roman Catholic.

Furthermore, even if we limit ourselves to the Gospels, two other defects of the Pharisees are brought to light even more clearly than their hypocrisy. Judging from the Talmud, these defects menaced the Pharisees more consistently than did hypocrisy. One such defect was the Pharisees' excessive liking for casuistry. The other was a tendency to confuse what is essential with what is incidental, by placing both on the same plane: "Woe to you, blind guides, who say, 'If any one swears by the temple, it is nothing; but if any one swears by the gold of the temple, he is bound by his oath.' . . . 'If any one swears by the altar, it is nothing; but if any one swears by the gift that is on the altar, he is bound by his oath.' . . . you tithe mint and dill and cummin, and have neglected the weightier matters of the law, justice and mercy and faith; these you ought to have done, without neglecting the others. You blind guides, straining out a gnat and swallowing a camel" (Matt. 23:16-24). Even so, if we are to have a proper appreciation of the situation, these characteristics of Pharisaism must not be considered in isolation, but must be placed in their spiritual context.

Josephus tells us that the Pharisees are "a body of Jews with the reputation of excelling the rest of their nation in the observances of religion, and as exact exponents of the laws," and again, "the Pharisees . . . have the reputation of being unrivaled experts in their country's laws" (*Life* 28). This defines the very essence of the sect. The Pharisaic ideal resided in an exemplary piety centered on the law: on the one hand, in the diligent, tireless meditation on the law (night and day, said the rabbis); on the other hand, in the fulfilling of its injunctions. Each conditioned the other.

The Pharisee was above all a schoolman and a scholar. But the school was that of life, and study guided conduct. The law formed a whole. To be sure, a distinction can be made between the moral commandments and the ritual prescriptions. But they both express the divine will to the same degree. Thus there could never be a question of placing one over against the other, nor even of setting up a hierarchy of one over the other. Such a hierarchy did sometimes tend to be established, and in a way contrary to what we would expect. That is, occasionally the ritual aspects took precedence over the ethical. Yet this can be seen as a temptation that way lays every religion to the degree that it attempts to express itself outwardly.

However, the code of the Torah, which regulated both the individual and the collective life of the Jews, did not make provision for every possible situation. This was the task of the doctors of the law and their students. In the light of sacred Scripture, they were to fix the conduct to be followed in each indivdual case. The Pharisees' casuistry balanced on the edge of formalism, and sometimes fell over into it. It seems to us to have been overly meticulous and hairsplitting in the extreme. When we read of discussions on minute points, of quibbles, and of distinctions bordering on the ludicrous, we sometimes feel that we are in the presence of a sterile form of mental gymnastics. But this is only the perversion or the hypertrophy of an approach that was perfectly legitimate in itself. This approach was of vital importance for Pharisaism. In no way did it exclude spontaneous, sincere, and intense piety and the most authentic religious feeling. Admittedly, the pride of the Pharisee doctor and the Pharisee's contempt for the ignorant and sinful masses, coupled with the innumerable prescriptions of ritual purity with which the Pharisees surrounded themselves, fostered an exclusivist spirit in these "separated ones." This is why they organized themselves in small cells or confraternities (*haburoth*). Yet this was not all that there was to Pharisaism. The feeling of election was usually combined, here as elsewhere, with the feel ing of a task to fulfill. "Love the creatures and lead them to the law." Such was the fundamental principle of Hillel, one of the sect's most illustrious teachers. The Gospels themselves emphasize the missionary zeal of the Pharisees, who "traverse sea and land to make a single proselyte" (Matt. 23:15); and Josephus attests that the Sadducees have "the confidence of the wealthy alone but no following among the populace, while the Pharisees have the support of the masses" (*Ant.* 13.10.6).

The rivalry between the two sects can be viewed from several perspectives. For one thing, it was set within social categories: the Pharisees represented a sort of middle class over against the great priestly families. The rivalry was also, to a great degree, one of a difference of function, priestly on the one hand, rabbinical on the other. And this difference of function meant, finally, that the rivalry was between two religious institutions, the temple and the synagogue. It was not that the Pharisees repudiated the temple: according to Josephus, the prayers and the sacrifices were performed in accordance with the Pharisees' rubrics (*Ant.* 18.1.3). Nor were the Sadducees completely absent from the synagogue. Yet it is still true that the Sadducean caste controlled the liturgies of the one sanctuary, while the synagogue, the place of study and prayer, where the reading and the interpretation of the law were indissolubly linked to acts of worship properly so-called, was perfectly expressive of the Pharisaic conception of religion. The influence of Pharisaism was more and more widely disseminated throughout Palestine and the diaspora through the synagogues. This already established network, which had previously sustained the religious life of Israel, enabled Judaism to overcome the crisis following the destruction of the temple quickly and, apparently, easily. During the very course of the siege of Jerusalem, Johanan ben Zakkai, the age's most illustrious doctor of the law, succeeded in leaving the beleaguered city and obtained authorization from Titus to go to Jabneh (Jamnia) and open a rabbinical school, thus assuring for centuries the future of his religion.

Oral Tradition

We learn from Josephus that "the Pharisees had passed on to the people certain regulations handed down by former generations and not recorded in the law of Moses" (*Ant.* 13.10.6). This was, he explains, a subject of permanent dissension between the Sadducees and the Pharisees.

Indeed, it was essentially on this point that the two sects were in opposition. Whereas the Sadducees held to the letter of the written text, the Pharisees, from the sole fact that they interpreted the text, were quite naturally led to go beyond it, to qualify it, to enrich it. In their eyes, the tradition that they invoked in doing this, far from opposing the Torah, was the natural prolongation and explication of it. This tradition went back to Moses himself, just as did the Torah. An oral law was revealed to Moses along with the written law, and this oral law was faithfully transmitted from generation to generation. The rabbinical treatise *Aboth* ("The Fathers") formulates this Pharisaic theory of tradition and retraces the unbroken chain which, beginning with the lawgiver, linked each succeeding generation of doctors: "Moses received the Law from Sinai and committed it to Joshua, and Joshua to the elders, and the elders to the Prophets; and the Prophets committed it to the men of the Great Synagogue" *(Aboth* 1:1 ff.).[3] Then comes the enumeration of several pairs of teachers ("Antigonus of Soko received the Law from Simeon the Just, etc."), whose historical existence is more or less certain. The list finally ends with Hillel and Shammai, famous leaders of schools (Beth Hillel and Beth Shammai). The text devotes a few comments to each of these real or fabricated leaders of the Pharisaic line, summing up the oral teaching that they dispensed, along with their exegetical work on the written Torah.

This oral tradition, running from generation to generation and from school to school, finally ended by being committed to writing, in the Mishnah and the Talmud. It was then fixed, as it were, and became the subject of the exegetical efforts of succeeding generations. But before arriving at this point, the idea of tradition had been a factor of development, of adaptation, and even, at least in certain cases, of progress in the religious life of Israel. It made Pharisaism

---

[3] [Quotations from *The Mishnah* are taken from the translation of Herbert Danby (London: Oxford University Press, 1933).]

the living element of official Judaism. It was the tradition that allowed the Pharisees to justify all the elaborations that they introduced regarding the scriptural precepts, on the level of observances as well as on the level of doctrine.

In the matter of ritual, the Pharisees' position was characterized in general by their custom of multiplying prescriptions, particularly those dealing with ritual purity. According to the maxim attributed by the treatise *Aboth* to the "men of the Great Synagogue" (the ancestors, perhaps mythical, of the Pharisees, who appealed to them in order to secure their own place in the sun), this ritual purity involved making "a fence around the Law" *(Aboth* 1:1). To us, this supererogation often seems withering and deadening. Yet to the Pharisees it was the condition and the very source of all authentic religious life. The multiplicity of commandments, far from being resented as an intolerable yoke, on the contrary both revealed and called forth the multiplicity of divine blessings. Indeed, it was the inflexible rigor of observance that assured the survival of Judaism.

On the other hand, it is very significant that these rigorists, preoccupied with isolating themselves from the outside world, which they considered impure, should have made a place in their teachings for ideas obviously foreign to the ancient Hebrew foundations. Yet the paradox and contradiction are only apparent. The Pharisees were able to be more receptive on the doctrinal level precisely because the fence that they erected around the law sheltered them from a true syncretism. It should be added that both the movement which led them to enrich the unadorned biblical creed and their multiplication of commandments proceeded basically from the same tendency: in both cases they moved forward, beyond the written text.

Pharisaic Theology

Josephus says very little concerning the beliefs of Pharisaism: "What [reason] prescribes to them as good for them, they do; and they think that they ought earnestly to strive to observe reason's dictates for practice" (*Ant.* 18.1.3).[4]

Josephus' reference to the rationalism of the Pharisees should be taken with a grain of salt. To be sure, it should be understood that the rabbinical discussions, theoretically carried on with rational arguments, played a basic role in the elaboration of the Pharisees' guiding principles of life. So once again we are dealing primarily with practice. But the following is an example of the "rational" doctrine of the Pharisees: "Though they postulate that everything is brought about by fate, still they do not deprive the human will of the pursuit of what is in man's power

---

[4] [Thus Whiston's translation. Feldman's translation in the Loeb Classical Library reads: "They follow the guidance of that which their doctrine [*logos*] has selected and transmitted as good, attaching the chief importance to the observance of those commandments which it has seen fit to dictate to them." The translator comments that *logos* "would seem to have the same meaning here" that it does in the opening sentences of the sections (18.1.4-5) that present the views of the Sadducees and the Essenes, where Whiston gives the rendering "doctrine."]

. . ." (*Ant.* 18.1.3). Or again, ". . . that to act rightly or otherwise rests, indeed, for the most part with men, but that in each action Fate cooperates" (*War* 2.8.14). It is difficult to reconcile these two propositions, one of which, in the language of Christian theology, asserts the primary role of predestination, while the other gives a large place to free will. Concerned as always with speaking a philosophical language familiar to his Greek readers, Josephus has succeeded only in making things more obscure. It is also possible that Josephus, wanting at any cost to show an opposition between Sadducees and Pharisees, found such an opposition where none existed. Thus he becomes entangled in his own explanations. With the aid of our other sources, we can salvage some pertinent information from Josephus' confused comments, namely, that the Pharisees asserted with equal force the universal sovereignty of God and providence, on the one hand, and the possibility of man's finding or rejecting his salvation, on the other hand. Rabbi Akiba said, "All is foreseen, but freedom of choice is given" (*Aboth* 3:16). In any case, it is rather doubtful that the Pharisees had ever spent much time discussing these problems from a purely metaphysical standpoint. Josephus has hellenized them to the extreme, just as he did the Sadducees.

Josephus is somewhat more explicit and faithful when he speaks of the Pharisaic teachings regarding life after death: "They believe that souls have power to survive death and that there are rewards or punishments under the earth for those who have lived lives of virtue or vice: eternal imprisonment is the lot of evil souls, while the good souls receive an easy passage to a new life" (*Ant.* 18.1.3). Again, "Every soul, they maintain, is imperishable, but the soul of the good alone passes into another body, while the souls of the wicked suffer eternal punishment" (*War* 2.8. 14). Were we to take this last quote literally, we would be tempted to think that the Pharisees believed in reincarnation. Now, this is obviously not what is meant. The phrase "another body" undoubtedly refers to the body of those who will be resurrected.[5] Thus Josephus considers that only the righteous are entitled to resurrection. Jewish thought was very hesitant on this point, but it is certain that only a few teachers of the age taught a general resurrection of all men prior to the last judgment. Consequently, Josephus' testimony corresponds to the opinion held most widely among the Pharisees of his time.

Resurrection, whether universal or limited to the elect, was one of the key items of Pharisaic doctrine. The New Testament, as well as the rabbinical texts, corroborates what Josephus says on this subject. Moreover, it gives us further details concerning Pharisaic beliefs: ". . . the Sadducees say that there is no resurrection, nor angel, nor spirit; but the Pharisees acknowledge them all" (Acts 23:8). Angelology and demonology were not exclusively Pharisaic concerns, since they were found throughout the Judaism of the time (except among the Sadducees). Nevertheless, preoccupation with angels and demons was one of the

---

[5] [Cf. *War* 3.8.5; *Against Apion* 2.30.]

principal characteristics of the sect.

Genuine Pharisees always succeeded in reconciling belief in angels and demons with the strictest monotheism. But in other sectors of Judaism contact with the Gentile world brought a considerable blurring of the distinctions between Creator and creatures. On the periphery of Judaism, on the sometimes indistinct boundaries separating Judaism from paganism, we catch glimpses of sectarian groups (in the modern and exact sense of "sect") that never quite succeeded in resisting the temptation either of polytheism or of dualism. Of course, these groups were not representative of authentic Judaism. Yet we should remember that such groups existed, even though we shall not concern ourselves with a detailed description of them.

Even among the Pharisees the concern with angels (who were divided into distinct categories, the principal angels being known by name) inclined toward astrological and magical speculation; relationships between the celestial bands and the heavenly bodies were quite readily drawn. It is not improbable that Josephus, when he speaks of the sovereignty of fate, is covertly referring to speculations of this type. Although such speculations never flourished in an official way in the Pharisaic schools themselves, they were certainly present in the intellectual milieu of the day. On this level, intercourse among religions inevitably is established, no matter how exclusive the religions might be. The magic-tinged documents from the beginning of our era attest to the Jewish contributions to pagan magic.

Conversely, Israel received elements from paganism, despite its efforts to resist such contributions. It was undoubtedly from the Jews that primitive Christianity borrowed the idea that the pagan gods were really demons that could be utilized, should the occasion arise, for good or evil ends. It is generally admitted that the whole of postbiblical Judaism, insofar as doctrine was concerned, came under the influence of the surrounding civilization. This seems to have been especially true of Pharisaism: angelology, demonology, eschatology, and doctrines relating to the other world, all reflect in varying degrees the contribution of Persia in particular and of Mazdaism, filtered, adapted, and molded according to the needs of monotheism.

Furthermore, on all these points, as well as in the matter of practice, Pharisaism was far from achieving a perfect uniformity. Differences that were sometimes considerable existed among the various rabbinical schools. The observance of the law was sometimes strictly enjoined; sometimes more latitude in observance was permitted. This was the classic opposition between the schools of Hillel and Shammai, an opposition that is encountered again and again throughout the rabbinical period. Yet beyond the rivalries of the schools and the doctrinal quarrels, Pharisees of all stripes were linked by their conception of a religion more concerned with practice than with pure theological speculation, and by an equal respect for the doctor of the law, the expounder of Torah and the medium of the transmission of tradition.

Eschatology and Messianism

This rapid survey of Pharisaism would be incomplete were no mention made of eschatology and of messianic beliefs. Josephus says nothing of these matters, and for good reason. Writing after the national disaster of A.D. 70, of which he was an eyewitness, he undoubtedly had no illusions about the future. Even if he had, it would have seemed preferable not to dwell on those elements of Jewish belief that most disturbed the Greco-Roman mind and the imperial authorities. But we should not be led astray by his silence: messianic hope was still alive, quite alive indeed. It was this hope that was to incite, less than three-quarters of a century later, the second Jewish rebellion (132-135), led by the messiah Bar Cochba and crushed by the Emperor Hadrian.

It is difficult to say whether the Pharisees were the real source of this messianic hope or if, on the contrary, they merely shared it. Although it is present in certain of the texts that seem to have come directly from Pharisaic circles (for example, the collection called the Psalms of Solomon), it is also expressed in many other documents whose sources are less easy to determine (for instance, certain of the apocryphal and pseudepigraphical writings, among others).

In any case, this messianic hope was not the exclusive privilege of the Pharisees and was present far beyond the boundaries of that sect. Rare was the Jew who was not grasped to some extent by this hope.

With the possible exception of the Sadducees, it was the common possession of all Israel and perhaps the major characteristic of Jewish religiosity of that day. This study on the sects and their characteristics is therefore not the place to give a detailed analysis of messianic hope. Suffice it to say that the Pharisees seemed to have awaited, with complete and unanimous (although short-lived) optimism, the return of the exiles to the Holy Land, the crumbling of foreign domination, the extermination of the impious, in short, the advent of the kingdom of Messiah—the peaceful and prosperous prelude to the final events and to the establishing of the "world to come."

Yet although all their hopes were keyed to the realization of these elating prospects, they did not feel called upon to hasten the time by taking a hand in events. Thus they were not militant to the point of messianic agitation. If there was such it was on personal initiative and not as a group. Such a case would be that of the Pharisee Zadok. When Judea was reduced to a Roman province in A.D. 6-7, Zadok joined the quickly suppressed revolt of Judas the Galilean.

Zealots

It was Judas who brought about the formation of the Zealot movement. Josephus lists the Zealots with the Pharisees, Sadducees, and Essenes as a school of philosophy. He undoubtedly does them an honor. He also presents Judas the Galilean as a very skillful sophist. The Zealots, Josephus says, had nothing in common with the other groups (*War* 2.8.1), which does not hinder him from stating elsewhere that the Zealots and the Pharisees were in agreement on all points, except that the Zealots professed a fierce attachment to liberty, recognizing God alone as master, and were always ready to suffer torture and death rather than bow before the authority of any man (*Ant.* 18.1.6). In this period, the authority in question was that of the despised foreigner; thus the Zealots, perhaps even more than anarchists, were intransigent nationalists. For them, politics and religion were inextricably interwoven. The theocracy of which they dreamed was simply their own law imposed on the country. In this respect, they did indeed represent the militant wing of the Pharisees. They expressed in actions a hostility that, in the Pharisees, most often remained theoretical. They firmly believed that God would intervene, but felt it their duty to make the first moves.

Josephus obviously did not like the Zealots, and blamed them for all the evils that beset Palestine during this period. Perhaps, in wanting to clear both the Romans and the Jewish people as a whole of responsibility, Josephus found it too easy to use the Zealots as scapegoats.

A recent book[6] has attempted an interesting rehabilitation of the Zealots. According to W. R. Farmer, the Zealots were noble patriots who have been unduly

---

[6] W. R. Farmer, *Maccabees, Zealots, and Josephus* (New York: Columbia University Press, 1956).

debased to the status of cutthroats; in reality, says Farmer, they were the true successors of the Maccabees. This is going a bit too far. In particular, this theory fails to understand the very real difference between the aggressive and intolerant policy of the forced Hellenization of Palestine, such as that attempted by Antiochus Epiphanes, and the Roman domination. The latter was indeed accompanied by the blunders and vexatious measures of procurators who were often uncomprehending, malevolent, and brutal. Yet under the Romans there was never any serious question concerning the right of the Jews to practice their religion, which was a *religio licita* in the empire. The mere presence of the Romans, irregardless of their acts, was enough to make the Zealots rise up against them. There is no doubt that this revolt was religiously motivated, but it was a religion of illuminati and fanatics.

The antipathy which these people inspired in Josephus, who was a pro-Roman bourgeois, perhaps led him to paint them a bit too somberly. Yet it is difficult to believe that he has completely distorted them. The wretchedness in which they lived probably had something to do with their agitation, which would thus be the expression, in certain respects, of the reaction of what could be called a proletariat, mainly rural. Social oppositions were called into play along with national and religious antagonisms. But whatever were their obviously complex motives, the Zealots were terrorists. Furthermore, they did not restrict their attacks to the Romans. They seem to have been quick to wield the knife, against the pagans of course, but also against the lukewarm among the Jews. These lukewarm, in the eyes of the Zealots, were not only quisling Jews, but also those who accepted the Roman occupation too complaisantly. Moreover, the Zealots' position appears to have progressively hardened. It is probable that all were not equally savage and that the "zeal" which motivated them was manifested with varying degrees of virulence according to the time or the region. But it can at least be said that they contributed greatly to the fostering, at the beginning of our era, of that chronic ferment which finally brought catastrophe to Palestine.

3

*The Dead
Sea Scrolls
and Essenism*

THE ESSENES, according to Josephus, were one of the three (or four, if we include the Zealots) Palestinian sects or schools of philosophy. Thus he considers them, along with the Pharisees and the Sadducees, authentic representatives of Judaism. I have already pointed out that this overly schematized viewpoint needs to be qualified. Whereas the Pharisees and the Sadducees together constituted official Judaism, in which their rivalry was the dominant factor, the Essenes were located on the fringes from the very first. The Essenes, like the Pharisees, had begun as a voluntarily segregated group. At the time of Christ the Essenes were still such a group, whereas the Pharisees had ceased to be such except in a relative fashion. The Essenes were separated from the masses, whom they considered to be impure and impious. They were separated from the Sadducees who, in their eyes, represented an illegitimate priesthood. They were separated from the Pharisees.

despite certain affinities of spirit, practice, and doctrine, because in general they exceeded the Pharisees in the strictness and the completeness of their observance of the law. They were separated from the Zealots, despite certain belated convergences (we shall come back to these later), because Essenism by nature was not at all a manifestation of militant nationalism. Indeed, the Essenes were separated from the totality of the Jews, because they constituted a closed society, with secret rites and esoteric teaching.

The Essenes have often been called a confraternity, i.e., a religious order. This is a valid definition if we do not forget that this order was also a sect. Troeltsch maintained that the sect is to Protestantism what the religious order is to Roman Catholicism, and that both express the same tendency toward separation (pushed to the extreme in one case, channeled and contained in the other). If this is true, then the Essenes participated at one and the same time in both of these sociological realities. Its structure was that of an order, its teaching and spirit those of a sect. A Roman Catholic order conceives of itself only in the framework of the church, where it accepts other categories as legitimate, for example, the clergy and the laity. The Essenes, on the contrary, "were, in their own eyes, and to the exclusion of all other Jews, representatives of the only Covenant agreeable to God. . . . the new community was the 'little remnant' foretold by the Prophets, i.e., the true Israel."[1]

---

[1] A. Dupont-Sommer, *The Essene Writings from Qumran*, trans. G. Vermès (Oxford: Basil Blackwell, and Cleveland: Meridian Books, 1962) , p. 42. Quotations from this volume © 1962 by the publishers, used by permission.

Thus the term "sect," when applied to the Essenes, has more of the meaning that we usually attribute to it than when it is applied to the Pharisees or the Sadducees.

The Meaning of "Essene"

Philo, who calls them Essenes (*Essaioi*), advances the theory that the name derives from the Greek *hosioi*, which means holy or pure.[2] Josephus, who vacillates between the forms *Essaioi* and *Essenoi*, suggests a similar but even more labored etymology, deriving *Essenoi* from *semnoi* ("the venerable"). It is obviously arbitrary to attempt to explain the name of the Essenes by utilizing the Greek. But it is not impossible that the term derives from the Aramaic equivalent of *hosios*, namely, *hasya*. It is true that this term is attested only in East Aramaic (Syriac), and not in that of Palestine (West Aramaic)[3]; thus we should perhaps seek the origins of the sect in the area of Mesopotamia. But it should also be pointed out that *hasya* (plural *hasen, hasayya*) is the equivalent of the Hebrew *hasid;* the word "Essenes" would thus be a transliteration (perhaps through Aramaic) of *hasidim*, "pious." Indeed, we have already seen that those who called themselves such during the Maccabean period were, in all probability, the ancestors of the Essenes.

---

[2] *Apology*, in Eusebius, *Praep. Ev.* 8.11.1.
[3] [But see on this point the comments of J. T. Milik, *Ten Years of Discovery in the Wilderness of Judaea*, ("Studies in Biblical Theology," No. 26; London: SCM, and Naperville: Allenson, 1959), p. 80, n. 1.]

On the other hand, the Mishnah (*Shekalim* 5:6) refers to a room in the Temple called the "Chamber of the Silent,"[4] *hasaim*, who have sometimes been identified with the Essenes; *hasaim* could, in fact, be transliterated into the Greek *Essaioi*. The rather farfetched way in which the Mishnah explains the name given to this room denotes simply the quandry of the redactor in face of a name that was no longer understood. It is not impossible that the room in question had some link with the Essenes, and that the practice of monastic silence had given rise to the nickname "the silent ones."

Recently, Dupont-Sommer has suggested that the word "Essene" is related to the Hebrew *ezah*, meaning "council" or "party."[5] The Essenes, then, would be men of the council (or party) of God, a phrase that is indeed found in the Qumran texts. But Dupont-Sommer himself recognizes that the exact etymology of the word remains uncertain. In reality, while none of the proposed explanations is improbable, neither does any one explanation assert itself with convincing force. For my part, I am more inclined to the view that the word derives from the Aramaic *hasya*.

The Library of Qumran

I have mentioned the Qumran texts. As recently as 1948 we knew the Essenes only through a few re-

---

[4] [In Danby's translation, "the Chamber of Secrets."]
[5] [Cf. *The Essene Writings*, p. 21, n. 3, and p. 43.]

marks made by Philo,[6] by Josephus,[7] and by Pliny the Elder.[8] But all at once our information was enormously enriched and renewed by the sensational discovery which brought to light the documents that are sometimes called the Dead Sea scrolls, sometimes the Qumran texts.

Much has been said and resaid on the circumstances surrounding the discovery, on the negotiations concerning the manuscripts, and on the sometimes roundabout course followed by the manuscripts before they finally reached the workshops where they could be deciphered. One spring day in 1947[9] a Bedouin, Muhammad adh-Dhib, while looking for a lost sheep, discovered a cave in a cliff about a mile and a quarter back from the shore near the northwest corner of the Dead Sea. The cave is within a mile of a place called Khirbet Qumran. Inside the cave, Muhammad adh-Dhib found eight earthenware jars, one of which contained scrolls. Clandestine excavations were carried on in the area by other Bedouins, and eventually a methodical search was made by the Jordan Department of Antiquities, the French Dominican School of Archeology, and the Palestine Archaeological Museum. In the years following more caves were discovered (at least eleven, including the first), bringing to

---

[6] *Every Good Man* 12.75-88; *Apology* (conserved in Eusebius, *Praep. Ev.* 8.11).

[7] *War* 2.8.2-13; *Ant.* 18.1.5.

[8] *Nat. Hist.* 5.15.

[9] [The date of the discovery has been challenged by the same Bedouin in a signed declaration published by W. H. Brownlee in *Journal of Near Eastern Studies*, 4 (1957), 296 ff. Cf., however, F. M. Cross, Jr., *The Ancient Library of Qumran* (rev. ed.; Garden City: Doubleday Anchor Books, 1961), pp. 5-6, n. 1].

light new scrolls and manuscript fragments. These documents have been acquired by institutions of learning in various countries. Many of the writings have been published, and the others will eventually be made available, some by the Hebrew University of Jerusalem, others by American institutions, and the remainder by an international team working in the Palestine Museum of Jerusalem (Jordanian Zone). Various translations have made them partially available to the public. The bibliography that they have given rise to has reached immense proportions; a catalogue published in 1957 already listed more than fifteen hundred titles, not including works of pure popularization. The list has not stopped growing. Indeed, in recent years a journal has been founded that deals exclusively with the Qumran texts and related matters (*Revue de Qumran*). The importance of the discovery is evident.

I shall not deal in detail with the description of the documents which constitute the "Library of Qumran." It will suffice to say that this now famous site has furnished both complete manuscripts and fragments (of very unequal importance) of all the books (with the sole exception of Esther) which made up the biblical canon of the Palestinian Jews at the time of Christ. Parts of certain writings (Tobit, Ecclesiasticus) have also been found that were accepted by the Alexandrian Jews (followed by the Roman Catholic Church) while being regarded as noncanonical by the Palestinian synagogue. The Pseudepigrapha of the Old Testament (Jubilees,

Enoch, Testaments of the Twelve Patriarchs) are also represented in the Qumran manuscripts. Finally, a number of manuscripts, composed by the members of the community, give us a picture of the organization and teachings of the sect of Qumran itself. These documents, which are more interesting for our purposes, are the Damascus (Zadokite) Document (known for over a half century from two manuscripts found in Cairo; fragments of this document have been identified at Qumran); the Society Manual,[10] which records the rules of the community; the Military Manual, which contains instructions for the eschatological combat of the sons of light against the sons of darkness; the liturgical Thanksgiving Hymns (*Hodayot*), and a series of commentaries on the biblical books, especially the Predictions of Habakkuk. A considerable number of other fragments attest to the existence of works of less interest or importance.

Such a harvest is without precedent. It sheds valuable light on the history of Hebrew writing and on the history of Jewish literature. As we shall see, it throws new light on the origins of Christianity. It brings alive, with a precision unequaled to the present, one of the Jewish sects of the beginning of our era.

There is very little doubt regarding either the dating of the texts or their authenticity. But although the authenticity of the texts raised scarcely any ques-

---

[10] [The nomenclature utilized for the documents from the first cave (1Q) is that proposed by W. H. Brownlee, *The Meaning of the Qumran Scrolls for the Bible* (New York: Oxford University Press, 1964) , pp. xix-xxi.]

tion, their dating originally gave rise to quite serious differences of opinion. Some scholars dated either the manuscripts as such or the composition of the writings (other than the biblical books) several centuries before the Christian era, while others placed them in the Byzantine age, or the period of Arab domination or, indeed, during the time of the first crusade. Archeology has succeeded in clearing up this point. In fact, it soon became evident that there was a link between the caves of manuscripts and the archeological site of Qumran. This site had been known previous to the discoveries, but it was not explored methodically until afterward, by the French School of Archeology of Jerusalem. Excavations uncovered the ruins of a complex of buildings. The nature of this complex of buildings is undeniably communal and conventual, but it was not designed to shelter a very large number of occupants. The size of the adjacent cemetery, however, presupposes a sizable population. Consequently, a considerable part of the community must have lived in the surrounding area, in huts and caves in the cliff. Among other rooms in the monastery, there was a scriptorium where the manuscripts were copied. Undoubtedly, some of the manuscripts were already deposited in the caves, at the disposition of the hermits who lived there. But eventually, under circumstances that can be reconstructed with only partial certainty, the whole library of the monastery was hidden in the caves.

The buildings of the community show very definite traces of violent destruction. Besides, the coins found at Qumran cover the period between the end of the second century B.C. and A.D. 68. It is clear, therefore, that the history of the Qumran sect terminated with the Jewish revolt of A.D. 66-70. It was at this time that the caves were used to hide the books of the community. Thus none of the writings could be later than this tragic episode of Palestinian history. All of the writings were either pre-Christian or contemporaneous with the birth of Christianity. On this point, the agreement of specialists is now almost unanimous.

The Identity of the Qumran Covenanters

Some differences of opinion remain concerning the identification of the Qumran sectarians.[11] However, these differences have diminished considerably since the initial controversies raised by the discoveries. Many of the proposed identifications were found to be untenable when the chronological problem was resolved.

For example, it is no longer possible to identify the Qumran group as Karaites, who were latecomers on the Jewish scene, although there does seem to be a certain dependence of the latter on the former.

There are also certain striking affinities between the Qumran sectarians and the first Christians, in organization, ritual, and spirit. This has led some scholars to identify the Qumran group with the primi-

---

[11] [For a list of some of the theories of identification and those scholars who propose these theories, see H. H. Rowley, *From Moses to Qumran* (New York: Association Press, 1963), p. 239, n. 3, and p. 241, notes *a* and 2.]

tive church or, more precisely, with its Judaizing branch, the Jewish-Christian Ebionites. In this view, the Teacher of Righteousness venerated by the sect would be Jesus Christ himself. I shall come back at the appropriate time to the analogies between the two groups and the two figures. These analogies are sufficiently precise to call for an explanation; they are not sufficiently precise to authorize the proposed identification.

The Sadducean hypothesis is as tenuous as the Jewish-Christian hypothesis. It rests almost exclusively on the term "sons of Zadok" with which the Qumran men designated themselves. I have already pointed out, in regard to the Sadducees, how we should understand this term: by claiming that they were descendants of the high priest Zadok, the sectarians undoubtedly were affirming that they were the only legitimate priesthood, over against the pretensions of the Jerusalemite caste. In reality, the Qumran group and the Sadducees were in almost total opposition on most points.

Other scholars have identified the Qumran group with the Pharisees. The affinities are indeed more precise, and could very well express common origins. In particular, what we know of the Pharisaic cells or *haburoth,* cannot help but remind us of the Essene community. Nevertheless, it is evident that the Qumran group went beyond all the norms of Pharisaic legalism. As I have already emphasized, the Qumran group remained separate from the rest of Israel at the very time that Pharisaism, leaving its initial isolation, was in the process of identifying itself with Judaism (or at least was remodeling Judaism in its own image). The people of Qumran were ascetics and anchorites, the Pharisees were not.

Finally, the British historian Cecil Roth has suggested that the Qumran sectarians were Zealots.[12] His thesis is developed with agility, but it scarcely stands up under analysis. It necessitates compressing the life of the group into a very short period, the few years of the Judean war. Thus the group would have composed all of its writings and copied all of its manuscripts during the very time that it was waging a merciless combat against the Romans. The identification of personages proposed by Roth is completely unacceptable. Furthermore, in a more general way, the few items of information which Josephus gives us regarding the Zealots are not in accord with the texts of Qumran.

These attempts, and other less important or even more tenuous theories that need not be mentioned here, all have one error in common: they single out one or two characteristics from the general picture given by the texts and isolate these characteristics arbitrarily and artificially from the whole. But if we examine the entire picture, correlating all the literary, historical, and archeological data, and if we compare the Dead Sea scrolls with the observations

---

[12] [Cecil Roth, *The Historical Background of the Dead Sea Scrolls* (New York: Philosophical Library, 1959). This view was also proposed by H. E. del Medico, *The Riddle of the Scrolls* (London: Burke, 1958). For criticisms of this view, see Dupont-Sommer, *The Essene Writings*, pp. 397-403; R. de Vaux, "Les manuscrits de Qumran et l'archéologie," *RB*, 66 (1959), 87-110.]

given by Philo, Josephus, and Pliny then we are inevitably led to conclude that the people of Qumran were Essenes. The Essene theory, developed by Dupont-Sommer and other specialists shortly after the publication of the first manuscripts, has received an increasingly large number of adherents. The overwhelming majority of critics now hold to the Essene theory.

The demonstration of this thesis has been repeated many times, and I shall not reproduce it in detail. Without mentioning the many convergences between the ancient authors and the newly discovered texts, two major arguments seem to me to establish incontestably the validity of the Essene theory. First of all, the Qumran documents bring alive before us a group whose rigorously communal nature is striking. Among the sects described by Josephus, only the Essenes are presented as a true community. The information of Philo furnishes the same picture: ". . . they dwell together in communities . . . they all have a single treasury and common disbursements; their clothes are held in common and also their food through their institution of public meals. In no other community can we find the custom of sharing roof, life and board more firmly established in actual practice" *(Every Good Man* 12.85-86).

Of course, it can be objected that neither Josephus nor, especially, Philo has given an absolutely complete picture of the Judaism of his time and that consequently the people of Qumran could be identified with some more obscure sect, one not mentioned by either Philo or Josephus. But this is where the second argument becomes pertinent—that of a geographical nature.

Pliny the Elder locates the Essene sect with remarkable precision: "On the west side of the Dead Sea, but out of range of the noxious exhalations of the coast, is the solitary tribe of the Essenes . . ." (*Nat. Hist.* 5.15). After briefly describing their characteristics, he continues: "Lying below the Essenes [*infra hos*] was formerly the town of Engedi . . . Next comes Masada, a fortress on a rock . . ." *(loc. cit.).* These geographical designations coincide perfectly with those of the Qumran site, which is located on a terrace overlooking and set back a bit from the western shore of the Dead Sea. It should also be observed that in Pliny the word *infra* means "downstream" rather than "lower down." The ancients considered the Dead Sea as the prolongation of the Jordan Valley, so that Engedi and Masada, situated further south, would indeed be "downstream" from Qumran. Since it cannot be contested that the newly discovered buildings are of a monastic type, it is inconceivable that two different and important monastic communities could have existed together on the narrow strip of land between the banks of the Dead Sea and the western cliffs without Pliny's making some allusion to both. Since he knows of only one cenobitic "people" in that region, whom he calls Essenes, and since the Qumran site corresponds exactly with the type of life described briefly by Pliny and in more detail by Philo and Josephus, we are surely justified in considering this site as an Essene settlement, undoubtedly the "mother house" of the order.

Considering this convergence of literary, archeological, and geographical proofs and clues, the few remaining difficulties are of little weight. Yet we should at least mention them and try to resolve them.

First of all, the term "Essene" itself (or its Hebrew equivalent) never appears in the Qumran texts. The sect refers to itself with various names: the Many, the Poor, the sons of Zadok, the community of the covenant, (or of the new covenant), or simply the community, the sons of light, etc. It is surprising that among all these various appellations we never come across the vocable utilized by our classic sources, namely, "Essenes." However, we should remember that the term "Christian" is absent both from the Gospels and from the Pauline epistles, and that the disciples of Christ were first designated as Nazarenes (Hebrew *nozrim*), which remains their normal appellation in the Jewish circles of Semitic tongue (the Christians applied this term exclusively to a Jewish-Christian sect). Nor should we forget that the word "Essene" is only the Greek transliteration, more or less apt and more or less faithful, of a Hebrew or Aramaic term that we are not able to identify with complete certainty. Perhaps it should be viewed as a nickname given the sectarians by outsiders. If, on the contrary, we want to relate the name to a term which the sectarians applied to themselves, we should consider, among the various etymologies proposed, either *hasya-hasid*, or *ezah* (council); indeed, the

Qumran texts refer to the sect here and there as "the Holy" or "the Pious" and as the "People of the Council of God."

Another difficulty is Pliny's insistance that the Essene group "has no women and has renounced all sexual desire" (*Nat. Hist.* 5.15), and that no one is born into the sect (*gens in qua nemo nascitur*); it is renewed only by the continuous influx of recruits converted to the Essenes' ascetic ideal. Philo, for his part, tells us that the Essenes "eschew marriage [and] practice continence" (*Apology* 8.11.14). According to Josephus, "They disdain marriage for themselves, but adopt the children of others . . ." (*War* 2.8.2). However, one or two tombs excavated in the cemetery adjacent to the monastery of Qumran, which was undoubtedly the communal cemetery, contained skeletons of women. This discovery accords with certain of the texts which take into account the sect's married members, their wives and their children, and formulates precise rules concerning marriage. This discovery also contradicts the information given by Pliny. Josephus, it is true, in addition to his account of the monks dedicated to celibacy, knows of "another order of Essenes who, although in agreement with the others on the way of life, usages, and customs, are separated from them on the subject of marriage. Indeed, they believe that people who do not marry cut off a very important part of life, namely, the propagation of the species" (*War* 2.8.13). This has generally been felt to imply a sort of "third order," striving to live the Essenian ideal "in the world," in the very heart of the cities.

But on the basis of the new witness that we have in the texts, it must be admitted that married members were present at Qumran itself, at least during certain periods of the sect's history. It is difficult to determine whether they were fully integrated into the community life or whether, on the contrary, they were located near the monastery, following a somewhat less strict rule. It is not impossible that there was a feminine branch of the order, although the texts make no mention of it. Such was the case with the Therapeutae, Jewish monks of Egypt, who present certain similarities with the Essenes. Finally, the suggestion proposed by Dupont-Sommer is not without merit, namely, that "in some exceptional case a pious woman may have been admitted to take her last sleep in the cemetery of the holy ascetics,"[18] even during the period when only celibate monks were at Qumran. Thus many solutions can be proposed to the problem. In any case, the presence of women at Qumran does not constitute a decisive objection to the Essenian character of the community.

The same is true for another point, namely, the pacifism of the Essenes. "As for darts, javelins, daggers, or the helmet, breastplate or shield, you could not find a single manufacturer of them, nor, in general, any persons making weapons or engines or plying any industry concerned with war, nor, indeed, any of the peaceful kind, which easily lapse into vice" (*Every Good Man* 12.78). Josephus presents them as "peacemakers." To illustrate their strength of char-

---

[18] *The Essene Writings,* p. 65.

acter, their heroism, and their scorn of death, he describes the tortures they smilingly suffered during "the war against the Romans" (undoubtedly that of A.D. 66-70); but he is apparently speaking of innocent and passive victims and not of belligerents. That is to say, the Essenes described by Josephus were not tortured for having revolted against the occupying forces; rather, they suffered torture for having refused to blaspheme the Lawgiver or to eat forbidden food (*War* 2.8.10).

Such a picture is in complete contrast with the spirit and letter of certain Qumran texts, notably the Military Manual. This work, by an anonymous member of the Community, sets forth precise details of the strategy for the final conflict in which, evidently, the Essenes intended to play a role. To be sure, it can be objected that what is involved in these texts is nothing more than eschatological visions or a purely literary exercise in the line of the apocalypses of the age, with no relationship to any reality whatever. It is nonetheless true that the very complacency with which the author envisages these warlike prospects seems unexpected enough when compared with the ancient testimony to the pacifism of the Essenes. The existence of this writing has given the proponents of the Zealot theory one of their weightiest arguments, one which is worth considering. An explanation is required for the apparent contradiction between Essenism as we have known it up to the present time and the texts of Qumran.

It is possible that Josephus and Philo were only

imperfectly informed concerning the sect, which they viewed from the outside. The Essenian teaching was enclosed in the greatest secrecy, and Josephus and Philo could have missed many of the characteristics of this teaching. It is also quite possible that they wanted to overlook certain elements of the Essene teaching. This suspicion is especially applicable to Josephus. As we have already seen, he quite willingly accommodated Jewish realities to the Greco-Roman fancy. His liking for the Romans, coupled with his professed admiration for the Essenes, would have forbidden him to regard the Essenes as the representatives of that aggressive nationalism which he so distinctly condemned in the Zealots. It is not certain that the Essenes were as foreign to the Zealot outlook as Josephus makes them out to be. It is Josephus who numbers a certain John the Essene among the leaders of the revolt of A.D. 66-70 (*War* 2.20.4 and 3.2.1). Was John the only one to take up arms, and did he do it against the will of the sect? Were all of the Essene martyrs mentioned previously quite as innocent, from the Roman point of view, as Josephus implies? In view of the particularly tragic circumstances of that time, it would not be surprising to find that the sect was affected by the nationalistic contagion which was spread throughout many sectors of the Jewish people, giving rise to the idea of a holy war against the impious. In falling in with this nationalistic fervor, the Essenes would only have been resuming contact with their first origins, since the *hasidim* ("the pious") who rose up with Judas Maccabeus were, in all probability, the direct ancestors of the Essenes.

Furthermore (and this remark is valid not only concerning the question of pacifism, but for all the points on which perfect agreement does not exist between the data of the scrolls and the data of the ancient authors), it is quite likely that the sect did not remain always and everywhere unchanging. Even when we consider only the texts of the community itself, the picture that is presented differs according to whether we consult, for example, the Damascus Document or the Society Manual. These divergencies undoubtedly derive from the simple fact that our various sources have reference to different ramifications of the Essene movement or to successive periods in its development. Pliny is the only one to locate the Essenes on the Dead Sea. From that we could conclude that their principal settlement was there. But Philo tells us that they lived in "many villages" and were grouped in "great societies of many members" (*Apology* 8.11.1). (The plural should be noted.) Josephus is even more explicit: "They are not in one town only, but in every town several of them form a colony" (*War* 2.8.4). It could be the case that these different settlements corresponded to certain variations in ritual, belief, or behavior. Perhaps the question of marriage was not the only one to give rise to different modes of obedience among the Essenes. It is inconceivable, especially, that the sect had not varied with the times and had remained immutably fixed in the same positions throughout its history. The fluctuations of the history of Palestine itself could have brought forth alternating phases of pacifism and of bellicose fanaticism. Thus the problem is to locate these phases in relation to one another. It is here, on the chronology of the sect and of its writings, that we could well use some precise details that are sorely missing. Dupont-Sommer had originally assigned the Military Manual to the period of the Seleucid dynasty, "perhaps during the very times of Judas Maccabeus." This date has also been proposed by other authors. More recently, however, Dupont-Sommer has placed the date of composition after the arrival of the Romans (63 B.C.).[14] The work seems to him to reflect the period when the sect, "persecuted by the High Priest Hyrcanus II, was intoxicated with the hope of vengeance." In any case, the writing would belong to a relatively ancient phase of the history of the Essenes, who would later have settled down to docility "to the authority of Rome and its representatives." Thus the picture painted by Philo and by Josephus would correspond quite well with the situation at that time. J. T. Milik, on the other hand, maintains that the Military Manual was composed "shortly after the death of Herod, at a time when tension between Jews and the Roman authorities was mounting," and thinks it likely that "at the signal for the outburst of the Revolt the Essenes left Qumran, after hiding their manuscripts away in caves, and joined the ranks of those who were fighting the Romans . . . ."[15] Consequently, in sketching a hypothetical "history of the Essenes," Milik distinguishes a phase (the fourth and last) which spans the

---

[14] Cf. *The Essene Writings*, p. 167.
[15] *Ten Years of Discovery*, pp. 122, 123.

period from Herod (d. 4 B.C.) to the first Jewish Revolt (A.D. 67-70). This phase he designates as "Essenism with Zealot tendencies." Thus the accounts of Philo and Josephus concerning the pacifism of the Essenes need to be retouched. Their accounts would correspond with a state of things that had already disappeared when they were writing.

It is difficult to choose between these two opposing theories. Both have the merit of resolving the contradiction between the classic remarks concerning the Essenes and the Qumran texts. Both theories are backed up with valid arguments. Yet neither one has absolutely compelling force. This is a disappointing conclusion, but it is a conclusion that must be made each time we confront the solutions proposed for the various problems raised by the Dead Sea scrolls. The dates and order of the writings, the major stages in the history of the group, the events which marked its history, the identity of the personages who shaped the history all too often remain obscure. The difficulty comes from the very nature and literary genre of the texts, which were usually composed in the veiled, symbolic, and esoteric language dear to the apocalypses of the time. Such apocalyptic writings had very little concern for precise dates and names. While they were undoubtedly comprehensible to those for whom they were originally destined, their precise meaning frequently eludes twentieth-century readers.

In particular, it would seem to be impossible, given the present state of the available evidence, to identify the mysterious figure of the Teacher of Righteousness, who occupies considerable space in the scrolls and whom the Qumran sect venerated as its founder or, at least, as its principal source of inspiration.

Roger Goossens has suggested that the Teacher was Onias the Just,[16] who lived during the time of Pompey's occupation of Palestine (Onias is known both from Josephus and from the Talmud). But this identification raises quite serious difficulties and has found few supporters. In fact, it is very difficult to locate the Teacher in any particular period. To do so, we must first clarify the identity of another figure, the "Wicked Priest," the adversary and persecutor of the Teacher and his followers. This Wicked Priest was undoubtedly one of the Hasmonean sovereigns, but which one is unclear. Many names have been proposed, including Jonathan (160-142 B.C.), Alexander Jannaeus (103-76 B.C.), and Hyrcanus II (76-67, 63-40 B.C.). It is also a possibility that the figure of the Wicked Priest was a composite of traits borrowed from various historical personages. Furthermore, the Qumran sect evidently was plagued and hounded by several of the Hasmonean kings, and the writings which allude to these events could have been reworked along the way.

The same is true for the biblical term "Kittim." This term, borrowed from the Book of Daniel, is utilized in the Predictions of Habakkuk to designate the Romans. Yet in the more ancient of the Qumran

---

[16] [See, for example, Roger Goossens, "Onias le Juste, le Messie de la Nouvelle Alliance, lapidé à Jérusalem en 65 av. J.-C.," *La Nouvelle Clio*, no. 7 (July, 1950), 336-353. Also, Dupont-Sommer, *The Essene Writings*, p. 359.]

documents the term could well have been applied to other categories of enemies, the Seleucid armies, for example.

Again, the same can be said for the expression "the new covenant in the land of Damascus," which the Damascus Document utilizes to refer to the community. According to most scholars, this phrase denotes a real exile of the sect in Syria, during a period that cannot be determined with any precision. Yet it is also possible that "the land of Damascus" is an allegorical expression, meaning simply the desert of Qumran, a land of exile in relation to Jerusalem.

In the final analysis, it is difficult to date exactly the birth of the Qumran group as a distinct sect, due to the lack of sufficiently certain and irrefutable chronological reference points (of course, the first origins of the movement that eventually gave rise to Essenism are to be located at the time of the Maccabean revolt). In particular, much uncertainty exists concerning the dating of the Teacher of Righteousness. All that can be said is that he should be placed sometime between the middle of the second and the beginning of the first century B.C. Some doubt also remains concerning the circumstances of his death. It is possible, indeed probable, that he died a martyr, although this is by no means absolutely certain. In this respect, the documents resist all efforts of scholars to interpret them. Moreover, the Hebrew syntax of the texts is so flexible that a given phrase from the Predictions of Habakkuk, for instance, will be applied by some scholars to the Teacher of Righteousness, while

others apply it to the Wicked Priest (which, need-
less to say, would considerably modify the perspectives).

Yet no matter how serious these differences of
opinion might be, they have only relative importance
regarding the growing consensus on the principal
aspects of the problem. The remaining obscurities
are inconsiderable when viewed alongside the posi-
tive understanding that we have concerning the Qumran sect.

Rites and Practices of the Qumran Community

As a matter of fact, the Essenes have come alive
under our very eyes, so to speak. Up before dawn,
they began the day with prayer, which they recited
facing the sun, "as though entreating it to rise." Then,
according to Josephus, "the superiors dismiss them so
that each man may attend to the craft with which he
is familiar" (*War* 2.8.5). As Philo expresses it, "Some of
them labour on the land and others pursue such crafts
as co-operate with peace" (*Every Good Man* 12.76).
An oasis grew up around springs in the area, and the
cultivation of palm trees (mentioned by Pliny) undoubtedly constituted one of the essential resources
of the community. The group probably engaged in
the raising of some small livestock as well. Slightly
south of Qumran, in a place called Ain Feshka, excavations have uncovered the remains of an agricultural
and industrial complex dependent on the main
monastery. Among other buildings, it included a

tannery. The two sites offered all that was necessary for the various activities of the monks: "We have found a carefully planned hydraulic system (with reservoirs, aqueducts, and canals all linked together, settling tanks, cisterns, and communal basins); workshops for the production of the utensils and food necessary for a community living mainly in economic isolation (i.e., pottery, smithy, bakery, mill, and food stores); rooms and equipment for communal use (laundry, kitchens, refectory, assembly halls). . . ."[17]

After the midday meal, which was eaten in common, work continued until the evening meal. Liturgical gatherings, devoted to prayer and to the reading and explication of the sacred writings, occupied a "third of the night" (i.e., the whole evening) and the sabbath day, during which all profane activities were halted, including the fulfilling of natural needs.

The cohesion and harmonious life of the group was assured by a respected hierarchy, a strict discipline, the absence of private property, and community of goods. As I have already emphasized, the structure of the community was sacerdotal. The priests held a preponderant position. They were the "sons of Aaron," the "sons of Zadok." Assisted by the Levites, they presided over all gatherings and activities of a religious nature. Laymen, however, were in the majority, perhaps the great majority. They were represented in the council, which directed the community and managed its goods. They were "the people," the "sons of Israel." In certain cases, the entire community ("the Many"),

---

[17] Milik, *op. cit.*, p. 56.

gathered in general assembly, exercised judicial powers and decreed punishments against those who had transgressed the rule (the punishments could go as far as exclusion—temporary or definitive—or capital punishment).

Each postulant underwent a probationary period of one year, followed by a two year novitiate.[18] The steps in his progressive induction were marked by the donning of white linen (the costume of the order), by ritual bathing and, finally, by admission to the communion meal. Thus, at the end of three years of preparation, he became a full-fledged member. But before being admitted he was required to vow solemnly before his brethren to practice piety and to observe justice, obedience, and all the other virtues prescribed by the law of Moses and the rule of the sect. Furthermore, according to Josephus, the postulant swore "to conceal nothing from the members of the sect, and to reveal nothing to outsiders even though violence unto death be used against him. In addition, he swore to transmit none of the doctrines except as he received them, abstaining from all alteration, and to preserve the books of their sect likewise, as also the names of the Angels" (*War* 2.8.7). This passage clearly underlines the esoteric nature of the sect, and the texts themselves present quite the same picture.

The Essenian rites were, basically, those codified in

---

[18] [Several scholars (e.g., Burrows, F. M. Cross) assert that the text in question (Society Manual) has only a two-year preparatory period, the three-year figure coming from Josephus' misunderstanding of his source. F. M. Cross, Jr.. *The Ancient Library of Qumran*, p. 86, n. 61, and M. Burrows, *The Dead Sea Scrolls* (New York: Viking, 1955) , p. 234.]

the Torah. As far as the form was concerned, the rites were exactly the same as those in ordinary Jewish usage, especially in the usage of the Pharisaic synagogue. But practiced in a closed society, in this desert community, the rites acquired a distinctive meaning. Although the principal feasts were the same at Qumran as in the rest of Israel, others were added which seem to have been unique to the sect. Moreover, the complete liturgical cycle seems to have been set up according to a calendar which was different from the official Jerusalem calendar.[19]

The calendar of Jerusalem counted twelve lunar months of twenty-nine or thirty days each (354 days in each year). This required an intercalation of days during certain months and of a month in certain years, so as to make up the difference between the lunar year and the solar year. The calendar which was followed at Qumran (cf. the Book of Jubilees) contained 364 days (a number divisible by seven), divided into twelve months of thirty days each, with an intercalation of one day each third month. Each quarter thus had exactly thirteen weeks. The week was the basic unit. The major feasts fell on the same day of the week, year after year: New Year, Passover, and the Feast of Tabernacles came on Wednesday, the Feast of Weeks (Pentecost) on Sunday, the Day of Atonement on Friday. Such a computation closely follows that presupposed by the so-called Priestly

---

[19] [On the calendar of Jubilees (and its possibilities for modern calendar reform), see W. H. Brownlee, *The Meaning of the Qumran Scrolls,* pp. 46-47 and n. 2; J. Finegan, *Handbook of Biblical Chronology* (Princeton: Princeton University Press, 1964), pp. 49-57.]

school of biblical writings (Ezekiel, the redactors of the Pentateuch, Chronicles). Thus there is reason to believe that the calendar of Jubilees represents the ancient liturgical computation of the temple itself, which was later abandoned at Jerusalem in favor of the lunar-solar calendar in use in the Hellenistic world. It is not impossible that this substitution gave rise to the Essene secession. At least it would have contributed to their feeling that the Jerusalemite priests were impious and sacrilegious and that their own clergy was the only legitimate one.

Indeed, it does not seem that the temple played an appreciable role in the religious life of the Essenes. Philo explicitly states that they offered no sacrifice of animals (*Every Good Man* 12.75). Josephus, in a passage that is somewhat difficult to interpret, is less clear: "They send votive offerings to the temple, but perform their sacrifices employing a different ritual of purification" (*Ant.* 18.1.5). It is difficult to reconcile these two testimonies. Perhaps we should assume that on this point, once again, the attitude of the Essenes varied from time to time and from place to place. The temple is not formally condemned in the Qumran documents; certain texts accept the legitimacy of sacrificial worship. But since sacrificial worship, in the eyes of the sectarians, was sullied by the presence of an impure priesthood, it is probable that they did not value it very highly. That is, they were not hostile to sacrificial worship in principle, but because of the circumstances. Perhaps they actually offered sacrifices at Qumran itself, despite the law, which forbade the offering of sacrifice anywhere but in the temple of Jerusalem. It is also possible that Josephus used the term "sacrifice" metaphorically, intending by it only the rites peculiar to the sect. As we have seen, in describing Essene sacrifices he mentions their "purifications." Indeed, we know that these purifications took on considerable importance among the Essenes. A ritual bathing preceded each day's communal meal. Apparently this was adopted from the priestly ritual at Jerusalem, which obliged the priests to bathe themselves several times during the day, before and after cultic acts and especially before the evening meal, when they consumed what was reserved for them from the sacrificed meat. Furthermore, every stain, even involuntary, was to be erased by an ablution. Thus, in this respect, the Essenes went beyond normal Jewish practice and even beyond that of Pharisaism.

Initiation itself also involved a baptism, which cannot always be clearly distinguished in the texts from the daily lustrations: perhaps the baptism of new members consisted simply of admitting them for the first time to the normal immersions of the sect. In any case, it is certain that ritual purity was not the only thing involved in the Essenian ablutions. Purification was regarded as real and complete only if it is also moral; ritual was efficacious only if accompanied and confirmed by repentance: the sinner "shall not be absolved by atonement, nor purified by lustral waters, nor sanctified by seas and rivers, nor cleansed by all the waters of washing. Unclean, unclean shall he be for as long as he scorns the ordinances of God and allows not himself to be taught by the Community of His Council. . . . By his soul's humility towards all the precepts of God shall his flesh be cleansed when sprinkled with lustral water and sanctified with flowing water" (Society Manual 3:4-9).[20] Thus not only does water replace the expiatory fire of sacrifice, the ritual bath symbolizes the communication of salvation. That is, it has the value of a sacrament.

Moreover, we can say that the daily communal meal apparently constituted the fundamental act of the group's liturgical life. As we have seen, it marked the supreme degree of initiation. After bathing themselves in cold water, the Essenes, according to Josephus, "assemble in a special building to which no one is admitted who is not of the same faith; they themselves only enter the refectory if they are pure, as though into a holy precinct. When they are quietly seated, the baker serves out the loaves of bread in order, and the cook serves only one bowlful of one dish to each man. Before the meal the priest says a prayer and no one is permitted to taste the food before the prayer; and after they have eaten the meal he recites another prayer. At the beginning and at the end they bless God as the giver of life" (*War* 2.8.5). The Qumran documents confirm and augment

<hr>

[20] [The quotations from the various scrolls are taken from the Dupont-Sommer and Vermès translation, *The Essene Writings,* and are used with the permission of the publishers, Basil Blackwell, Oxford, and World Publishing Co., Cleveland. In translating Dupont-Sommer's work, G. Vermès has utilized the Hebrew and Aramaic texts in conjunction with Dupont-Sommer's French translation; Vermès has since published his own translation of the scrolls under the title *The Dead Sea Scrolls in English* (Baltimore: Penguin Books, 1962) .]

this testimony: "And in every place where there are ten persons of the Council of the Community, let there not lack among them a man who is a priest. And let them ask their advice in everything. And then when they set the table to eat, or prepare the wine to drink, the priest shall first stretch out his hand to pronounce a blessing on the first-fruits of bread and wine" (Society Manual 6:3-5).

To be sure, such a rite has parallels and perhaps even its source in the Jewish domestic liturgy where the meals were punctuated by blessings pronounced over the bread and wine by the father of the family. But it is clear that at Qumran these gestures took on a new meaning. The Essenian meal had a precise cultic nature. This is evidenced, in the comments of Josephus, by the preliminary purification, by the characteristic of sacred enclosure attributed to the communal refectory, and by forbidding the uninitiated to take part in the common meal. This cultic significance of the meal is underscored in the Society Manual by the requirement that a priest be present and by the principle that there be a minimum of ten participants. This latter is the well-known rule of *minyan*, which in rabbinical Judaism governed the synagogal cultic assemblies. If one is tempted to see the Essenian meal as a simple communal meal, like those of Christian monasteries, it should be pointed out that the latter can invite the heterodox or unbelievers to eat with them, whereas participation in the Eucharist is the privilege only of those who are actually Catholics. It appears certain that the Essenian refectory, where only the members of the group could enter, was the chapel as well as the dining room.

In addition, another Qumran scroll clarifies the profound meaning of the rite. It describes the organization of the community of the elect at the end of time and, more precisely, the meal to which they will be invited. This meal will be presided over by the Messiah of Aaron, of the tribe of Levi, the eschatological High Priest, spiritual leader of the community. Another personage will be seated after him, in second place. This is the Messiah of Israel, of the tribe of Judah, the political leader of the redeemed nation. "It is [the Priest] who shall bless the first-fruits of bread and wine, and shall first stretch out his hand over the bread. And afterwards, the Messiah of Israel shall stretch out his hands over the bread. And afterwards, all the Congregation of the Community shall bless, each according to his rank. And they shall proceed according to this rite at every meal where at least ten persons are assembled" (Society Manual Annex 2:19-22). Apparently this is simply the customary Essenian ritual, transposed into an eschatological framework. Consequently, we are justified in assuming that the daily cultic meal of Qumran is an anticipation of the messianic banquet, in the same way that the whole organization of the Essene sect is a prefiguration of the coming kingdom.

Qumran Theology

This brings us to the beliefs of the sect. Both Josephus and Philo, always anxious to gain a better

78

reception among their pagan readers, paid little attention to this eschatological aspect of Jewish hope. Thus neither one spoke of the messianic speculations of the Essenes. Philo, after having emphasized that they indulged in allegorical exegesis, presents them as specialists in theoretical and applied ethics. The information that he provides on this point accords with the information of the Qumran documents. Josephus analyzes in detail the Essenes' ideas on the soul and on the afterlife. He does this in terms of Greek philosophy. The body is corruptible, the soul is immortal. Emanating from "subtlest ether," the soul is imprisoned in the body until the time when death will free it from the bonds of the flesh. The souls of the just then go "beyond the Ocean," to a place of delights which the author compares to the isles of the blessed. The souls of the bad, however, are punished in a "dark pit shaken by storms," which Josephus identifies with Hades (*War* 2.8.11). The Christian writer Hippolytus, in a passage based on Josephus' observations, adds that the Essenes taught the resurrection of the body, final judgment, and a universal conflagration (*Refutation* 9.27). With the addition of these further details, the comments of Josephus are not, after all, improbable, even though they clothe the Essenes in Greek garb (or more precisely, in Pythagorean garb).

The Qumran documents show that the Essenes did indeed bring in foreign contributions to enrich the meager biblical data regarding the afterlife. Influences from Greek mystical philosophy are at least plausible, although they do not appear explicitly in the Qumran texts. On the other hand, it is quite difficult to explain the famous section Instruction on the Two Spirits (Society Manual 3:13-4:26) without making reference to Zoroastrian influences. The ideas contained in this work are emphatically dualistic, both cosmically and psychologically. The entire universe, as well as the human soul, is the theater of a merciless conflict, where the Angel of darkness is arrayed against the Prince of light. The cohorts of the spirits, good or bad, fight at their sides, contending until the final end, for the empire of the world and of men. "Dominion over all the sons of righteousness is in the hand of the Prince of light; they walk in the ways of light. All dominion over the sons of perversity is in the hand of the Angel of darkness; they walk in the ways of darkness" (Society Manual 3:20-21). The former will receive "eternal joy in perpetual life, and the glorious crown and garment of honor in everlasting light" (4:7-8). The latter will go into the "everlasting Pit [the dark pit mentioned by Josephus] . . . of unending dread and shame without end, and of the disgrace of destruction by the fire of the regions of darkness" (4:12-13). In the final episode of this drama, the Spirit of perversity himself will be banished.

Of course, all of this was put into terms that accorded with the demands of monotheism: not only would the final victory remain with God, it was God himself who "allotted unto man two Spirits that he should walk in them until the time of His Visitation"

(3:18). God is the origin and the end of all things. Similar views undoubtedly existed in other sectors of Judaism (which was not unaffected, in varying degrees, by Persian influences). The Essenes, however, developed these foreign ideas with exceptional vigor. For biblical thought and for ordinary Judaism, the omnipotent sovereignty of God was an already present fact. But the Manual, more than any other document, emphasizes with dramatic intensity the tension which dominates the history of the world from start to finish. In this respect, no other document gives the impression that the forces of good and the forces of evil fight with nearly equal weapons and that, up to the final moment, everything hangs in the balance.

This dualist perspective provides a framework for elucidating the details of Essenian ideology: (1) the place given to good and bad angels and to the names of the angels (the use of these names will mobilize or neutralize the spirits that bear them); (2) astrological speculations which teach "the physical characteristics of people born under a given sign of the Zodiac, and the exact proportion of their share in the world of the Spirits of Light, and in that of the Spirits of Darkness"[21]; (3) ethical teachings, based on a radical opposition of duly catalogued virtues and vices; (4) the sectarians' very Mazdean horror of any form of falsehood (5) a strict asceticism, which was the practical application of the dualist principle according to which the flesh, as the receptacle and aid of evil powers, must be rendered harm-

---

[21] Milik, *op. cit.*, p. 119.

less; and (6) the very organization of the community, "the remnant of Israel," the "militia" in the service of the Spirit of light; isolated from all impure contacts and from all pernicious influences in the fortress of its esoteric exclusivism, the community offers a prefiguration of the kingdom to come.

The Essenes, in fact, claimed a new covenant, and there is scarcely any doubt about the eschatological significance of the term. To aid in its inauguration, the Essenes prepared themselves, in penitence, for the final trials. The times were near. The coming of the Prophet, foretold by Moses (Deut. 18:15), would be preceded by the coming of the two Messiahs, of Aaron and of Israel. The Messiah of Aaron is sometimes designated in the scrolls as the Teacher of Righteousness. Perhaps this identical use of names overlaps an identity of persons, that is, it is probable that the Essenes awaited the return of their founder as the High Priest of messianic times, not limiting his role exclusively to the past. The expectation of his parousia would accord perfectly with the veneration with which they remembered him, a veneration which raised him to the same level as Moses himself, since God made known to the Teacher of Righteousness "all the Mysteries of the words of His servants the Prophets" (Predictions of Habakkuk 7:4-5). Thus the Teacher of Righteousness is the possessor of a gnosis which, by a unique privilege, has revealed to him the secrets of the final age; in the words of the New Testament, he knows the day and the hour. In general, he appears as the mediator of the new covenant.

This is to say that the person of the Teacher of

Righteousness is of primary importance in the study of the Essenes. The mystery surrounding him, despite all the efforts of scholars, is thus all the more irritating. The identity of the Teacher of Righteousness escapes us, the circumstances of his life and death remain obscure. Yet his religious ideal takes on substance in the organization of the sect, and is expressed in a more precise fashion in the Thanksgiving Hymns, which are the reflection of Essenian spirituality. It is quite likely that some of these hymns are from the Teacher himself. One feels in these hymns the true spirit of the prophets. They speak of the divine power and mercy, of the misery of man, who finds his refuge and strength in God alone, of the imminence of decision, of the vocation of the Teacher, of the glorious destiny promised to his faithful. One finds in these hymns—and we shall return to this subject—along with elements of an ecclesiology and of a soteriology, strains which herald Christianity.

I give Thee thanks, O Adonai,
for Thou hast redeemed my soul from the Pit
and from Sheol of Abaddon Thou hast made me rise
    to everlasting heights,
and I have walked in an infinite plain!

And I knew there was hope
for him whom Thou hast shaped from the dust
for the everlasting assembly.
Thou hast cleansed the perverse spirit from great sin
that he might watch with the army of the Saints
and enter into communion with the congregation
    of the Sons of Heaven.
And Thou hast cast an everlasting destiny for man
in the company of the Spirits of Knowledge,
that he might praise Thy Name in joyful concord

and recount Thy marvels before all Thy works.

But I, creature of clay, what am I?
Kneaded with water, for what am I accounted?
And what is my strength?

. . . .

And at daybreak Thou hast appeared unto me in
    Thy might
and hast not covered with shame the face
of all them that inquired of me,
that gathered in Thy Covenant and heard me,
that walk in the way of Thy heart
and are ranked for Thee in the assembly of the Saints.
And Thou wilt give everlasting victory to their cause
and truth according to justice,
and Thou wilt not allow them to stray in the power
    of the wretched
according to the scheme which they have devised
    against them.
But Thou wilt put their fear upon Thy people
together with destruction for all the peoples of the
    lands,
to cut off at the time of Judgment all who transgress
    Thy word.

And through me Thou hast illumined the face of
    many
and caused them to grow until they are numberless;
for Thou hast given me to know Thy marvelous
    Mysteries
and hast manifested Thy power unto me in Thy
    marvelous counsel
and hast done wonders to many because of Thy
    glory and to make known Thy mighty works to
    all the living.
    —Thanksgiving Hymns, III, 19-24, and IV, 23-29

Such texts are of inestimable value for our knowledge of the sect itself, since they reveal the vitality of its legalism. They also enrich the religious literature of Israel with a priceless contribution.

4

Other Palestinian Sects

THE ESSENE group was very important, but
it was by no means the only representative of the complex, multifaceted, and fluid reality of marginal
Judaism. It was only one sect among many others.
To be sure, no other sect has, as far as we know,
bequeathed any of its writings to posterity. This is
why the Dead Sea scrolls have elicited such exceptional
interest. However, we should not ignore the other
information on Jewish sects which we possessed
before the discovery of the Qumran texts, no matter
how meager and obscure this information might be.
In the following examination of other Palestinian
sects, I will leave aside the various expressions of
Jewish Christianity and of Judaizing Christian
gnosticism, and deal only with the groups that were
already existent when the church came into being.

We are acquainted with these groups through the
writings of various ecclesiastical writers of antiquity.
Some of these writers have in fact preserved catalogues of the Jewish "heresies." In general, these
catalogues are scarcely more than lists of names,
and it is often difficult to attach any concrete reality

to them. The names are accompanied by commentaries only in the later and untrustworthy authors, like Epiphanius (d. A.D. 402).

These references call for various remarks. First of all, it should be pointed out that the number of sects enumerated varies from author to author (between six and ten) and that the diverse lists only partially overlap. The longer lists, which are also the most recent, are those of pseudo-Jerome and Isidore of Seville (eight and ten names respectively). This is not to imply, of course, that these two authors had acquired a knowledge of Judaism and of the vanished sects that was more precise in proportion to the time that had elapsed. They simply amalgamated, or amplified on their own initiative, the lists of their predecessors. The Herodians and the "scribes" mentioned by Epiphanius (*Panarion* 1.20; 1.14) undoubtedly never existed as sects. Both are mentioned in the New Testament (Matt. 22:16; Mark 3:6), and this is where the author has come across them. But the Herodians were probably nothing more than partisans of Herod or men in his pay. As far as the "scribes" are concerned, they represented a function rather than a sect. Thus, for what is essential, we can fall back on the more ancient lists. These are found in Justin Martyr (*Dialogue* 80:4) and in Hegesippus, quoted in Eusebius (*Eccl. Hist.* 4.22.7). Both authors are from the second century. Each one speaks of seven sects, which is a symbolic number and certainly arbitrary. Both mention the Pharisees and the Sadducees; Hegesippus also names the Essenes and the Samaritans. Added to these well-known sects are others whose identity is much less clear. In Hegesippus we find mention of the Galileans, the Hemerobaptists, and the Masbothei, while Justin refers to the Genistae, the Meristae, the Galileans, the Hellenians, and the Baptists. Add to these names the Nasaraioi described by Epiphanius, and we have assembled the essential elements of a picture which we must now attempt to clarify.

Galileans

I shall not attempt to identify the Galileans. Attention has been called to them recently by the discovery in the Judean wilderness of a letter from Bar Cochba (leader of the Jewish rebellion of A.D. 132-135) which mentions the Galileans. They have by turns been identified as an obscure sect located in Galilee, as the disciples of Judas the Galilean (that is, the Zealots) and, finally, as the Christians themselves. Julian the Apostate, in the fourth century, designated the Christians by this name, and it is not impossible that this was the name given them from the beginning, at least in certain Jewish circles. On this view, it was by inadvertence that the Christian writers, not having recognized their true identity, classified the Galileans among the pre-Christian Jewish sects. In my opinion, none of these interpretations is irresistibly convincing. It is better to admit our ignorance than to want to fix, at any cost, the meaning of a term that only new and more explicit documents will enable us to clarify.

Baptist Groups

The task is somewhat easier concerning the other groups mentioned in our lists. The Baptists and the Hemerobaptists were perhaps simply two ramifications of the same group or movement whose essential characteristic was the importance it attributed to the baptismal rite (probably a rite of initiation). In this regard, we should recall the baptism by immersion which Judaism required of its proselytes. It should also be pointed out that the Baptists practiced baptism not on converts from the Gentile world, to erase their congenital impurity, but on Jews. This would seem to imply that they considered their own coreligionists as impure, as well as the pagans. Thus we are indeed in the presence of a sect, in the precise meaning of the term. It erected a supplementary rite between itself and ordinary Israelites.

As for the Hemerobaptists, if their name is more than a simple synonym for the Baptists, it would seem to indicate that the baptismal rite was repeated by them each day, whereas the Baptists performed it once and for all. Perhaps the Hemerobaptists should be identified with the "morning baptizers" mentioned by the Talmud (*Berakoth* 22a). Finally, the term "Masbothei" is almost certainly the Greek rendering of an Aramaic doublet for the Baptists, and undoubtedly designates the same sect. Consequently, the Baptists should be distinguished from the Hemerobaptists, since Hegesippus mentions both Hemerobaptists and Masbothei.

Thus a first group of sects emerges from our texts. The aberrant nature of this group vis-à-vis the norms of official Judaism (Sadducean and even Pharisaic) seems to reside essentially in a ritualistic augmentation, even more emphasized in the Hemerobaptists than in the Baptists. Furthermore, the latter term seems to have been applied to a host of conventicles. These groupings were more or less diversified in their practices and undoubtedly also in their teaching (for it is impossible to disassociate rite entirely from doctrine). Yet all insisted on the importance of baptism, either once for all or repeated. It is not without reason that students of the period have spoken of a baptist movement existing in the region of the Jordan River around the beginning of the Christian era.

We know comparatively well one of the representatives of this movement, namely, John, called the Baptist, whose preaching was contemporaneous with that of Christ and concerning whom the Gospels give us important information.

John the Baptist led the life of a hermit and an ascetic in the wilderness of Judea. Clothed in a coat of camel's hair, his food was locusts and wild honey. A group of disciples gathered around him, fasting and learning formulas for prayer from their teacher. His message was that the kingdom of God was imminent and that in order to gain access to it one had to become worthy of it. According to the most widespread notion of the time, the inauguration of the messianic age was to mark the collective revenge of Israel upon the Gentiles. John the Baptist trampled these facile hopes. What counted was not that one belonged to the Chosen People; individual conduct was the decisive factor. The Jews, no less than the pagans, were subject to God's tribunal. John bluntly proclaimed this to the Jews: "You vipers' brood! Who warned you to escape from the coming retribution? . . . Do not presume to say to yourselves, 'We have Abraham for our father.' I tell you that God can make children for Abraham out of these stones here" (Matt. 3:7-9, NEB). Salvation lies in repentance. John called his hearers to abstain from all injustice, for the rich to give what they did not need to the poor, and for all, confessing their sins, to come and receive in the Jordan "baptism of repentance for the forgiveness of sins" (Luke 3:3). They could then await with a more confident heart the Day of the Lord and the Messiah of whom John was only the herald and the precursor: "He will baptize you with the Holy Spirit and with fire. His shovel is ready in his hand and he will winnow his threshing-floor; the wheat he will gather into his granary, but he will burn the chaff on a fire that can never go out" (Matt. 3:11-12, NEB).

The exact meaning of John's baptism has been much debated. Did it confer purity of heart, or did it only signify it? In other terms, did it have the efficacious value of a sacrament, in the Roman Catholic meaning of sacrament, or was it only a symbol? It is difficult to give a decisive answer to this question. In support of the first interpretation, one could invoke the formula defining the baptism:

"baptism of repentance for the forgiveness of sins."
This would seem to make it the very instrument of
divine pardon. But the fact that it presupposed repentance and confession of sins would accord better with
the second interpretation. The baptism of John
resembles proselyte baptism in the sense that it was
administered only once. But this formal analogy
seems to cover different meanings. Baptismal immersion conferred ritual purity on proselytes. In this
respect, it belongs to the repeated baths which marked
the religious life of the Jews themselves. To be sure,
ritual preoccupations were not completely absent in
John, but they are certainly not primary. His originality resided in the fact that he gave to baptism a meaning that was both ethical and eschatological, a meaning that was missing in both proselyte baptism and in
synagogal ablutions. Was it an efficacious instrument
or a symbol? Perhaps it was both. It is not certain that
the distinction was as clearly perceived then as it is
today. In any case, baptism had meaning only in
relation to the coming kingdom. It was, essentially,
the seal which marked the elect. It was the safe-con-
duct (indispensable if not sufficient by itself) for those
who wished to enter into the kingdom.

Such preaching collided headlong with the
accepted ideas. It struck directly at the easy con-
science of the parties in power, the Pharisees and the
Sadducees. According to the Gospel of Matthew, it
was against these men that the diatribe quoted above
was addressed. John's preaching, like all messianic
preaching, raised public unrest among the crowds

which flocked to the Jordan. This unrest was alarming to those in high places. Under the circumstances it is not surprising that Herod, tetrarch of Galilee, should intervene, since he was in charge of Perea where John was preaching. He had John arrested and imprisoned; then at the instigation of his wife, Herodias, he had the dangerous prophet beheaded.

The sect to which John had given life survived him briefly. In the New Testament we glimpse something of the rivalry between the first Christians and the followers of John the Baptist. The question was debated as to who was the greater, John or Jesus. Moreover, in the Book of Acts we learn that St. Paul, having encountered at Ephesus certain "disciples" who had received only the baptism of John, baptized them again "in the name of the Lord Jesus Christ," thus conferring the Holy Spirit on them (Acts 19: 1-7). Actually, it is probable that in many cases the followers of John were absorbed little by little into the nascent church. Some scholars have suggested that their distant descendants can be recognized in the sect of the Mandaeans, who still exist in lower Mesopotamia. But this attractive theory raises strong objections, and it is difficult to maintain it as such. In the final analysis, the preaching of John the Baptist would have been only one episode among many had not Jesus himself been influenced by it at the beginning of his ministry. It was on contact with John, and on receiving baptism at his hands, that Jesus became aware of his own vocation. The whole importance of the sect resides for us in that encounter.

Genistae and Meristae

Several scholars, working independently of one another, have arrived at the conclusion that the term "Genistae," which is obviously formed from the Greek *genos* ("kind," "species"), is the translation of the Hebrew *minim* (plural of *min*), which has the same meaning as *genos*. The rabbinical writings utilize the term *minim* to designate all, including the Christians, who deviated from the norms of the Pharisaic synagogue in matters of belief or ritual. Consequently, we are dealing with a very general term, the English equivalent of which would be "heretics." We are not in the presence here of a particular sect, as Justin believed.

Several explanations have been proposed regarding the Meristae, whose name is derived from the Greek *merizein* ("to divide," "to separate"). According to Isidore of Seville they were given the name because they admitted distinctions among the biblical books: *Separant Scripturas, non credentes omnibus prophetis, dicentes aliis et aliis spiritibus illos prophetasse* (*Etymologies* 8:4). Certain modern authors, on the contrary, give the term a reflexive meaning: the Meristae were those who separated themselves from the masses. Thus we would be dealing with nothing more than a Greek equivalent of *perushim* (Pharisees). Justin, through ignorance, would have artificially divided the most illustrious of the Jewish "sects." For my part, I have borrowed elements for a third explanation from Justin himself. In setting forth the Christian doctrine of the *logos,* Justin writes: ". . . This power was generated from the Father, by His power and will, but not by abscission, as if the substance of the Father were divided [*hos apomerizomenēs tēs tou patros ousias*]; as all other things, once they are divided and severed [*merizomena kai temnomena*], are not the same as they were before the division" (*Dialogue* 128).[1] Justin is obviously referring in this passage to certain heterodoxies which, by insisting too strongly on the substantiality of Christ the Logos and on his autonomy in relation to the Father, divided the divine essence and, at the extreme, preached two gods. Indeed, this is how Christian orthodoxy itself appeared to the Jews, who were poorly prepared to understand the difficult christological and trinitarian definitions and were therefore quick to see in these definitions a denial of the oneness of God. In the rabbinical writings there are frequent allusions to "another god" professed by heretics. There is no doubt that some of these allusions had Christianity in mind. But others, in equally obvious fashion, dealt with the deviations of Jewish thought itself. In fact, even before the church entered the picture, we catch glimpses of speculations in Jewish thought which endangered traditional monotheism. Undoubtedly, some Jews hypostasized a given divine attribute, or the ineffable Name, and individualized it to the extent of making it a distinct splendor of God. In my

---

[1] *Writings of Saint Justin Martyr,* trans. T. B. Falls ("The Fathers of the Church"; New York: Christian Heritage, 1948), pp. 347-348.

view, this was the case with the Meristae referred to by Justin.

This is apparently how we should interpret the statement of a gnostic writing recently discovered in Egypt, according to which "some Jews affirm that there is one God only, and others affirm that several gods exist."[2] Taken literally, this statement contradicts all that we know of Judaism from other sources. But if "several gods" refers to the personification of divine attributes and, moreover, if we admit that outside observers were susceptible to misunderstandings concerning the exact meaning and import of speculations on the question, then this statement becomes less unlikely. Furthermore, the developments of angelology tended to get embroiled with those of theology. It is probable that in certain circles more or less influenced by paganism the distinction between angels and gods sometimes became blurred to the point of disappearing. Particularly relevant in this regard is the case of the angel Yahoel, who is mentioned in certain mystical or apocalyptic documents from the beginning of the Christian era. His name is derived from the divine tetragrammaton, YHWH, which is often transcribed in Greek documents as Yaho. In The Apocalypse of Abraham, Yahoel is made to say: "I am called Yahoel . . . in virtue of the ineffable name that is dwelling in me."[3] This explains why he was sometimes designated as the

[2] Quoted in G. Quispel, "Christliche Gnosis und jüdische Heterodoxie," *Evangelische Theologie*, 14 (1954), 2.

[3] G. G. Scholem, *Major Trends in Jewish Mysticism* (3rd ed., rev.; New York: Schocken Books, 1954), p. 68.

"lesser Yaho," the lesser Yahweh. With this "other god," we are on the indistinct boundary between monotheism and polytheism. This example is only one among many, and it illustrates the receptivity (much greater than previously believed) of certain sectors of Judaism not only to the cultural influences of the surrounding world but also to gnostic speculations (to the extent that one can speak of a pre-Christian Jewish gnosticism).

If my interpretation is accepted, then one would be justified in concluding that the term "Genistae" (and perhaps also "Meristae") does not designate a well-defined grouping or a particular sect, but rather certain currents of thought or tendencies that were widespread and of diverse characteristics. Moreover, it is clear that Genistae had a broader meaning than Meristae, and included it: the Meristae were *ipso facto* Genistae.

In any event, vis-à-vis Pharisaism this heresy was doctrinal rather than ritual (as in the case of the Baptists). It did not reside in a voluntary segregation from the Israelite masses. Rather, at least in part, it lay in a state of mind that was particularly receptive to the influence of pagan thought.

Hellenians and Hellenists

Of course, the same thing can be said for the Hellenians as well. Various interpretations have been proposed, all presupposing a scribal error in the writing of the term (which would consequently require more or less arbitrary textual corrections). It seems to me that a more satisfactory explanation can be arrived at by taking the word as it stands. The term belongs to a whole series of Greek vocables ending in *-ianoi,* which are formed from substantives and designate the disciples or followers of someone. Examples would be *Kaisarianoi, Herodianoi,* and the most famous of all, *Christianoi.* The only difference (but it is an important one) is that *Hellenianoi* is not, like the other terms, formed on the proper name of a person. It is true that it could be derived from the name of Hellen (son of Deucalion), the mythic ancestor of the Greek race. However, it is more reasonable to relate it to the word *Hellene* in its ordinary meaning of "Greek." Thus the Hellenians would be those who followed or imitated the Hellenes, those who were enamored of Greek ways.

This brings us quite naturally to a similar term, namely, "Hellenists" (*Hellenistai*), which the Book of Acts uses to designate the followers of Stephen (Acts 6:1 ff.). The two endings *-ianos* and *-istes* are synonyms and sometimes interchangeable. For example, the disciples of Marcion are referred to by the Greek church fathers sometimes as *Markianoi* and sometimes as *Markianistai* (Justin, *Dialogue* 35; Eusebius, *Eccl. Hist.* 4.22.5). It is quite possible, in these circumstances, that the Hellenists of the Book of Acts and the Hellenians of Justin are one and the same group, or at least proceed from the same tendency. Moreover, and contrary to accepted opinion, the first term, Hellenists, must not be restricted to its purely linguistic meaning. The Hellenists of the Book of Acts were not distinguished from the "Hebrews" simply because they used the Greek language. Their name, like that of the Hellenians, sometimes had a pejorative connotation, and in the mouths of their adversaries it underscored the fact that they followed the Greeks, that is, the pagans. This was already the meaning attached to the term *Hellenismos* by the Second Book of Maccabees (4:13), and later, in Julian the Apostate, this was to become more or less the technical designation for paganism. To be sure, the verb *hellenizein* (from which is derived *Hellenistes*) means "to speak Greek," but it also means "to live and think in the Greek manner," just as *iudaizein,* in the vocabulary of ancient Christianity, meant "to live in the Jewish manner," "to judaize."

Thus the Hellenians and perhaps also the Hellenists received their name from the fact that they imitated the Greeks. In what did this imitation consist? One possible answer is that they attenuated the strictness of the commandments (especially the interdicts weighing on the relations between Israel and the Gentiles), and that, at the same time, their beliefs were more or less profoundly marked by influences from the Hellenistic world. It is also possible that the term, which is certainly pejorative, had only a very vague meaning. For the Jews of Palestine, the word "Greek" was a synonym for "pagan," *ergo* "impious." Also impious, in the eyes of the pious Jew (especially the Pharisee), was anyone in Israel who deviated on any given point from the faith and practice set by the Torah and tradition. Thus it is quite easy to understand how the "libertines" could be labeled Greeks or Hellenizers, even when their aberrations had only a very tenuous relation to Hellenism. If this is indeed the case, then the term "Hellenians" would not be a great deal more precise than "Genistae." Both would be general terms covering diverse realities, even to the point of including all the varieties of thought and practice outside of Pharisaism, which, even before A.D. 70, was tending to impose itself as the norm.

The Message of Stephen

If we desire more precision on this question, we must consider other documents. Once the Hellenians-Hellenists equivalence is admitted, then the Book of Acts provides invaluable help. Indeed, the message of the Hellenists appears with sufficient clarity through the speech (Acts 7:1-53) which the author of Acts puts in the mouth of their leader, Stephen. Furthermore, the substance of this speech is probably authentic.

The speech is essentially a vehement diatribe against the Jewish people (that is, official Judaism), which is eternally rebellious against the divine will. Stephen especially condemns the temple, which Solomon built in defiance of God's will: "However, the Most High does not live in houses made by men" (7:48, NEB). The meaning of such a statement becomes clear if it is remembered that in the usage of Hellenistic Judaism the word *cheiropoietos* ("made by man's hand") is more or less the technical designation for idols. In the Septuagint this term is often used to translate the Hebrew word *elil*, which means "idol." To reject the temple because it was made by human hands is thus to rank it together with idolatry. This condemnation almost certainly included the condemnation of sacrificial worship, of which the temple was the exclusive locus. It is significant that the only allusion which Stephen made to sacrifices was in regard to the golden calf, which he characterized also as "the thing their hands had made" (7:41, NEB). Stephen apparently saw no difference between the sacrifices offered to false gods and those offered in the temple, ostensibly to honor the Almighty. It is clear that in his eyes the development of ritual institutions since the desert period served only to illustrate a worsening apostasy. This apostasy took its point of departure in the worship of the golden calf, then manifested itself in the construction of the temple and the persecution of the prophets, and finally culminated in putting to death the "Righteous One," that is, Christ.

Apart from this brief allusion, Christ is not mentioned in the speech. This allusion could be omitted without taking anything essential from Stephen's message. On the other hand, Moses is central in the speech. His work is well distinguished from all which later falsified and distorted it. Apparently the role of Christ, at the time of his Second Coming, would consist essentially in restoring the Mosaic religion in all its original purity. He is the "prophet like me" foretold by Moses himself (Deut. 18:15, 18; Acts 7:37). Stephen and the Hellenists came to enlarge the ranks of the nascent church because they saw in Jesus' prediction of the destruction of the temple an echo of their own message, and because they saw in Jesus himself the previously anonymous prophet whom they awaited. But there is substantial reason for believing that their thought was already fixed in its basic outlines before they came into contact with Christianity. It seems to me that we are in the presence of a pre-Christian sect of reformist Jews, who preached a religion "in spirit and in truth."[4]

The Hellenists of the Book of Acts undoubtedly came from the diaspora. We are ignorant of the circumstances under which they later settled in Jerusalem. The term used to designate them had more than an exclusively linguistic meaning, but in the present case it was applied to Greek-speaking Jews. In addition, it is probable that the criticism raised by Stephen against the temple and its cult proceeded in part from that which certain Greek philosophers (and later Hellenistic Jewish thinkers) formulated against the pagan rites. In this respect, it is very significant that, according to Acts, the apostle Paul denounced classic paganism in the very terms employed by Stephen: "The God who made the world and everything in it, being Lord of heaven and earth, does not live in shrines made by man, nor is he served

---

[4] [For a detailed consideration of this question, cf. the author's *St. Stephen and the Hellenists in the Primitive Church* (London and New York: Longmans, Green and Co., 1958).]

by human hands . . " (Acts 17:24-25). This is a familiar theme of what could be called "spiritualist" polemic and of Judeo-Hellenistic apologetic. What is original in Stephen's speech is the way it pushes the argument to its logical conclusions and includes, in one and the same condemnation, the temples of idols and the sanctuary of Jerusalem (both of which are viewed as founded on the same motives).

"Heresies" of the same type, aiming at a more or less thorough purification of official Judaism, could arise and indeed did arise in Palestine as well. The witness of Epiphanius, although somewhat late, is of assistance here. The observations which he devotes to the Jewish sects have the advantage of being rather ample. But a great deal of caution is required in utilizing them, for he speaks of things in the past, and he does so with a regrettable absence of historical and critical spirit. Thus, for example, he classifies the Essenes among the Samaritan sects, while among the number of Jewish sects he lists a group which he calls the Ossenians (or Ossenes). Moreover, neither group corresponds with what we know of the Essenes from the most ancient sources. It is difficult, on this point as well as other points, to make a distinction between what is valid and what is pure fantasy. The information that derives from Epiphanius himself is relatively more useful with regard to what concerns the Christian or Jewish-Christian sects. It is, however, much less useful when it concerns pre-Christian Jewish groups. Rather than follow the example of many others and try to sift the remarks Epiphanius makes on the Jewish sects (the task would exceed the bounds of this small book, and would undoubtedly not lead anywhere), I will deal with only one example, which seems to have come from fairly reliable information. This example is that of the Nasaraioi (*Panarion* 1.18).

Nasaraioi

At first sight one would be tempted to consider the name as a simple doublet for "Nazarenes" (*Nazoraioi*), which is another transliteration of the Hebrew *nozrim*. However, Epiphanius, who uses the term *Nazoraioi* to designate a Jewish-Christian sect, has forestalled any identification between the two groups by saying that they had nothing in common. In fact, if we accept the etymology proposed by Lidszbarski (for whom the term means "observants"), it is possible that this name had been used of a pre-Christian group, then of the first Christians in general and perhaps other sects as well, later coming to designate the Jewish-Christians and also, finally, the Mandaeans.

Whatever view is taken regarding their name, the pre-Christian Nasaraioi were conspicuous for their very characteristic peculiarities. They were Jews by race. According to Epiphanius, they dwelt in Galaatides, Basanitides, and the other regions along the Jordan. They practiced circumcision, observed the sabbath and the other feasts of the Jews, and recognized the fathers mentioned in the Pentateuch as representatives of true religion. But although they acknowledged that Moses had indeed been given the divine law, they rejected the Pentateuch, for they denied that the authentic law was that found in the Pentateuch. Finally, while keeping all the observances of the Jews, they refused to offer sacrifices or to eat the flesh of animals. These things had been invented by Scripture and were not in use in the times of the patriarchs.

There is nothing in this description that could not be substantially accurate. Thus we are once again in the presence of "heresy" of ritual, since it is expressed both in a rejection of sacrifices and in a vegetarian diet. But these characteristics were accompanied by a repudiation of the official biblical canon (in whole or in part, and at least the Pentateuch itself), under the guise of a distinction between divine law and human commandments. Thus this heresy presupposes a concept of revelation that differed from both that of the Pharisees and that of the Samaritans. It is probable that the sectarians in question utilized either a Bible containing revised and expurgated versions of the canonical books, or esoteric scriptures that were entirely different from our Old Testament. The attitude that is attributed to them finds significant continuations in the history of Jewish-Christian thought.

For one thing, this attitude heralds the distinction which certain ecclesiastical texts of antiquity established between the first codification of the covenant, which was the genuine law (primarily of an ethical nature, and summarized by the Decalogue), and the second codification which followed the worshiping of the golden calf. This second codification was developed in the essentially ritualistic prescriptions of Leviticus and Deuteronomy, as the instrument of divine reprisals toward the sinful and idolatrous people.[5] Second, the message of Stephen, dealt with previously, derived from the same attitude. This message quite logically presupposed a purifying of the biblical writings: it is difficult to see how the Hellenists could denounce the temple and its cult as blasphemous while at the same time continuing to venerate as inspired those texts of the Old Testament which exalted the former and codified the latter.

Finally, the characteristics which Epiphanius attributes to the Nasaraioi reappear trait by trait in the Jewish-Christian sect of Ebionites. The only additions are faith in Christ and a somewhat peculiar Christology. (The Ebionites, described by Epiphanius, produced the original versions of the pseudo-Clementine writings). This group provides a particularly clear example of the mechanism involved when a Jewish sect passes over into Christian heterodoxy. Of course, we are ignorant of the circumstances in which this passing was effected. We can at least presuppose that it was related to the Palestinian catastrophe of A.D. 66-70. We know that at the beginning of the revolt the primitive Christian community was located at Jerusalem and soon removed to Pella in Transjordan. The first contacts between the two groups apparently were made at that time and place. Seeing the new

---

[5] Cf. M. Simon, *Verus Israel* (2nd ed.; Paris: de Boccard, 1964), pp. 114 ff.

arrivals, like themselves, escaping the catastrophe by virtue of a special protection from heaven, the Nazarene sectarians could have been led to concern themselves with the Christians' faith, with their ritual practices, and with the person of their Master. Thus the Ebionites would have discovered affinities, real or fancied, between his message and their own. Such affinities would have invited a fusion between the two sects. For it is probable that with the Ebionites, as with Stephen, the criticism of existing cultic institutions was combined with the expectation of an eschatological Prophet (perhaps identified with the Messiah) whose essential task would consist of re-establishing, in all its purity and for all the Jewish people, that genuine religion which, at least for the present, they alone practiced.

Thus a Jewish sect was able to fall in with Christianity and, although remaining on the fringes of ecclesiastical structures, change into a Jewish-Christian sect. But what was true in this case was also true before the emergence of Christianity: contacts undoubtedly existed also among certain Jewish groups of the periphery, on the fringes of the Pharisaic synagogue. There must sometimes have been rapprochements, alliances, and fusions, especially where geographical proximity obtained. The lack of documents means we can only conjecture concerning these other groups. Moreover, we do not know which of the sectarian tendencies carried the day, the properly sectarian tendency toward isolation and reciprocal excommunication or the tendency to join together in the face of the suspicious or aggressive hostility of the

Roman authority, of the priesthood, or of the Sanhedrin. We can disclose certain affinities between one group and another, and these affinities may sometimes express a common origin. This does not always necessarily imply that amicable relationships were present, as we are reminded by the recent history of Christian sects. "Nearest neighbors quarrel best," as the English proverb puts it.

Perhaps we will never know whether or not the Essenes, Baptists, Hellenists, and Nazarenes represented diverse branches of one and the same trunk, and whether their similarities are explained by this common origin or, on the contrary, are born of reciprocal influences. Perhaps we will never know if their differences are congenital or chronologically secondary. Certitude is lacking on the plane of history. On the phenomenological plane, however, things are clearer. Closely related from the start or born of analogous but independent causes, opposing one another or at least occasionally united, these conventicles which, in the face of the decline of the Sadducees and the ascendency of the Pharisees, constituted marginal Judaism, had in common the same rejection of "normative" Judaism, the same dissatisfaction with it, the same concern for reform. These "Genistae" of all persuasions expressed the same negative and critical reaction, that of the nonconformist, to the norms and tendencies of official piety and teaching. In this respect, they indeed belong to the same religious and sociological type as Christian dissentients of all ages, despite the fundamental differences between the two religions.

5

Alexandrian Judaism

AT THE BEGINNING of the Christian era, a relatively small proportion of the Israelite population lived in Palestine. A greater number of Jews lived in the diaspora, around the Mediterranean and even in Mesopotamia. In general, we know very little about their religious characteristics. The documents they have left us consist of a few inscriptions (mainly funereal, and not very informative) and of some decorated monuments, catacomb frescoes, and bas-reliefs. The inscriptions are of little help in clarifying the picture of this extra-Palestinian Judaism. The latter prove, at least, that the Jews of the diaspora were not entirely closed to the artistic tastes of the Greco-Roman world and that on occasion they adopted or adapted certain themes of the pagan iconographic repertory. On the other hand, we have no literary text that reveals to us what the Jews of Rome, Antioch, or Carthage thought and believed.

The only city on which we are better informed (but the exception is a brilliant one) is Alexandria. The origins of the Jewish colony go back almost to the founding of the city by Alexander; the colony grew in numbers continuously from that time. If we look only at numbers, it was Alexandria more than Jerusalem which figured as the capital of Israel around the time of Christ. An original tradition of Jewish thought and culture was developed there, which was expressed in an abundant literature. A considerable part of this literature has come down to us. Thus we are quite well acquainted with Alexandrian Judaism and are in a position to understand what differentiated it from the Palestinian forms of Judaism.

But is it proper to speak of sects in this regard? As I have already pointed out, the diaspora included certain sectarian groups, in the more modern and specific sense of the term, whose theological or cultic peculiarities clearly placed them outside the community of Israel. This was due to the fact that, in their compromising with paganism, they went too far beyond the limits fixed by the law and by a tradition that was even rather flexible. These sects were essentially syncretistic, undoubtedly composed of both paganizing Jews and Judaizing pagans. Thus these little-known conventicles are, by definition, beyond the scope of our inquiry, since we have limited ourselves to those groups or currents which, judged by the objective criteria of history, can be more or less justifiably presented as representative of authentic Judaism. The Alexandrian synagogue unquestionably measures up to these criteria. Along with the great Palestinian sects, it constituted one of the major branches of Judaism. There are no important differences, on the level of organization and practice, between it and the Judaism of the Pharisaic type. But philosophical and theological speculation occupied an exceptional place in Alexandrian Judaism, and therein lies its originality. It was indeed a school of thought, the most distinctive one of the Judaism of the time.

Egypt also gave rise to a particular form of Jewish monastic life, related to the Essenes, but not identified with them, namely, the Therapeutae.

Jewish-Alexandrian thought was characterized in general by a deliberate effort of synthesis between the data of biblical revelation and those of Greek philosophical thought. This effort was already apparent in the Greek version of the Bible (Septuagint), which was elaborated from the beginning of the third century B.C. for the benefit of those Jews who no longer understood the ancestral tongue. Apparently, the Septuagint quickly became the official Bible of Alexandrian Judaism. The peculiarities of the translation faithfully reflect the mentality and the preoccupations of those who made it and used it. One notices particularly the concern to eliminate the anthropomorphisms of the Hebrew text, to substitute a completely spiritual image of God who is the God of the universe and not simply of the Chosen People, to replace expressions or concepts that were too specifically Semitic with terms or ideas borrowed from Greek philosophical schools. Thus the Septuagint, at the same time that it expressed the Jews' effort to rethink their religion, also presented Judaism to the truth-seeking pagans, in a form they could understand.

Philo

This twofold preoccupation also inspired, in even more precise fashion, other manifestations of Jewish-Alexandrian religious thought, the most distinguished representative of which was Philo, a contemporary of Christ. Philo's voluminous literary production, which is largely extant, is the blossoming of the tradition born of the Septuagint. All we can do here is to give a brief analysis of the basic aspects of Philo's thought.

Philo was a believing and practicing Jew. His spiritual life was nourished by daily contact with the holy books. He accepted, without restriction or reservation, the idea of revelation, of the election of Israel, and all the commandments of the Torah down to the details. Indeed, those biblical books which most interest him, which he meditated on and commented on without ceasing, were the five books of Moses, i.e., the law in the precise meaning of the term. Philo's very universalism was based on the law, not on the message (extrapolated to include all humanity) of certain prophets. On first sight, such a position seems paradoxical, for the essential object of the Torah, the charter of the covenant concluded between God and Israel, is to isolate the holy people from all impious nations. This is envisaged especially in the ritual prescriptions of the Torah. In this respect, the Torah, when compared for example with Second Isaiah, presents the most particularist aspect of the Old Testament. But such was not Philo's view. For those who understand it, the Torah is not only the national and religious code of a people. It has universal, indeed cosmic, meaning and import. In fact, the Pentateuch opens on the story of the Creation, and this is needed to show that "the world is in harmony with the Law, and the Law with the world, and that the man who observes the law is constituted thereby a loyal citizen of the world" (*On the Creation* 1.3). In order to understand such an assertion, it is necessary to remember that at the start Philo postulates, and attempts to demonstrate, the perfect identity of the Mosaic precepts with the best elements in the teachings of the pagan philosophers, all of whom are dependent, in some degree, on the Bible as their primary source of inspiration. Furthermore, it is necessary to take into account the exegetical method which conditions all his thought, namely, the allegorical method.

Certain philosophers, the Stoics in particular, were upset or scandalized by the all too human visage and the frequently unedifying adventures attributed to the immortals. Consequently they tried to salvage something from the mythology by seeking a hidden meaning in the stories (even in the scabrous ones), and by seeing behind the divine figures either the forces or elements of nature, or intellectual or ethical concepts. Myth thus becomes allegory: Zeus was the vital principle, Poseidon the sea, Athena reason. Even before Philo, certain Alexandrian Jews had applied these same principles of interpretation to the Bible, either to respond to the objections of the pagans or to reinforce their own confidence in the sacred texts.

The *Letter of Aristeas* (second century A.D.) has recourse to this method of interpretation in order to explain certain peculiarities in the dietary prescriptions of the law. The practical utility of ritual observances, we are told, is to protect the holy people from impure contacts. But more than this, they also have a symbolic meaning, which constitutes a veritable moral teaching. Their object is to awaken pious thoughts and to form character. For example, the birds that the law permits one to eat are all gentle and peaceful, and are noted for their purity, since they nourish themselves on grain. On the contrary, the flesh of birds of prey must not be eaten, for they do violence to others and devour them. By designating birds of prey as impure, the Lawmaker wanted to indicate that we must cultivate justice and abstain from all violence. In the same way, the law permits one to eat the flesh of animals which are ruminants and which part the hoof and are cloven-footed (Lev. 11:3 ff.). Animals which do not present both of these characteristics cannot be eaten. The cloven foot and the parted hoof represent the distinction between good and evil. He who knows how to make this distinction has a faithful memory, which is symbolized by the fact of rumination. Permission to eat the flesh of ruminants which part the hoof is an aid to remembering the blessings of God and to distinguishing in every circumstance between good and evil (*Letter of Aristeas* 145-155).

The utilization of such a strange exegetical method in no way implies that one is freed from the burden of observance. On the contrary, it makes the burden acceptable because it is reasonable. Applied to mythology, allegorical exegesis dissolves the divine figures as such. Transposed to the Jewish law, it leaves the prescriptions of the law intact. The literal meaning remains. It is simply combined with a spiritual meaning, which clarifies it and makes it more precise, and at the same time reinforces the normative nature of the commandment. The *Letter of Aristeas* attempts, more or less felicitously, to provide the proof of allegory. Philo stresses it, although he unequivocally condemns its extreme practitioners (those who utilize it in order to throw observance overboard): "They ought to have given careful attention to both aims, to a more full and exact investigation of what is not seen and in what is seen to be stewards without reproach. . . . We should look on all of these outward observances as resembling the body, and their inner meaning as resembling the soul. It follows that, exactly as we have to take thought for the body, because it is the abode of the soul, so we must pay heed to the letter of the laws. If we keep and observe these, we shall gain a clearer conception of those things of which these are the symbols" (*Mig. Abr.* 16.89, 93).

Furthermore, Philo's allegorical exegesis was not applied only to the prescriptions of the law. It also included the narrative parts of the Bible. The reality of the personages which play a part in these narratives is not questioned, any more than was the obligation to observe the commandments. They were indeed historical figures, but at the same time they were also symbols of moral qualities or of metaphysical verities. Adam is the soul, which succumbs to temptation, represented by Eve. From Adam's fall is born pride (Cain), and consequently righteousness (Abel) is eliminated from the life of the soul. However, the soul can be exalted once again by hope (Enos), repentance (Enoch), justice (Noah), virtue (of which each patriarch represents an aspect), and complete holiness (Moses).

Thus Philo's distinction between the spirit and the letter of Scripture, the one giving life to the other, corresponds to the distinction between soul and body, which are different in nature, but, for the present, are interdependent. Moreover, there is a parallelism, and even an identity, between the destiny of the individual and the history of humanity (interpreted allegorically) as it is recounted in the Holy Book, from the fall of Adam to the pact which God concludes with Moses. It is each man's responsibility to retrace for himself this itinerary leading to God. By shaking off the rule of the passions, that is, of the flesh, man can enter upon this itinerary here below. For Philo's anthropology is itself a projection, in a sense, of his cosmology, which borrows from Plato the basic distinction between the intelligible world (that of ideas) and the sensible world, between spirit and matter. In turn, this cosmology furnished the groundwork for a dualistic ethic which culminated in a mysticism.

Just as the air is populated with incorporeal souls, so the incarnate human soul, aided by divine grace, must strive through the practice of wisdom and of a strict asceticism to reascend to that spiritual world from whence it came. By throwing off the bonds which matter lays upon it, and by freeing and nourishing the divine spark which indwells it, the soul will arrive at ecstasy, the supreme form of that knowledge of God which is the primary object of religion. This God is the God of the Bible: one comes to him by following the teachings of Moses, "the great mystagogue." But this God is also the Absolute Being spoken of by the philosophers. Philo himself speaks of him in terms borrowed from the Stoics, Aristotle, and especially Plato (whom Philo calls "great" and "most holy").

Philo dwelt at length on a problem which, although central to Platonic philosophy, seemingly was not a problem for biblical thought, namely, the problem of the relation between a perfect, transcendent God, who is pure spirit, and a world created by him yet nevertheless imperfect. Philo's thought is particularly difficult on this point. Diverse and contradictory interpretations have been proposed in this regard, undoubtedly because this element of Philo's thought is itself full of contradictions. Some of these contradictions are real, while others are only apparent (due to the fact that Philo occasionally used the same term to mean quite different things). Philo sometimes stretched the biblical data to fit the framework of philosophy. It would be risky to attempt to summarize this remarkable but perilous synthesis in a few words without falsifying it. We can however, give at least some of the essential elements of it.

Philo inserts a whole series of strictly ranked intermediaries between God and the sensible world. The *logoi*,[1] the intelligible archetypes of the creation, which are more or less clearly identical with the Platonic ideal forms, are also sometimes the angels, messengers, or mandatories of God. Over and above the ensemble of *logoi*, which are also called powers or potencies (*dunameis*), is a group of five major powers, which are also ranked according to a hierarchy. In ascending order, these include the power which forbids that which is evil, the commandment which prescribes that which is good, mercy, the royal power, and the creative power. These are, as it were, God's representatives in his relations with humanity and the world. In particular, they act on God's behalf in the biblical history and are manifested in the theophanies related in the sacred text.

At the summit of this pyramid of beings is the Logos. The Logos is, undoubtedly, the most elevated and the closest to God of all the individual *logoi*. But he is also a sort of collective being which includes all of them and from which they have emanated individually. In fact, the Logos embraces all beings, for he is properly the principle and organ of the creation and conservation of the universe, which has issued entirely from him. Philo calls him the firstborn of God, the highest in age of the angels, the image of God. He even designates him as God (*Theos*), without the article which qualifies the perfect Being (*ho Theos*).

---

[1] [The term *hoi logoi* is translated by G. H. Whitaker (in the Loeb Classical Library edition of *On the Creation*) as "principles or nuclei of things" (13.43 and note, p. 475).]

Participating in the divine nature, yet nevertheless inferior to God, the Logos has been given "the special prerogative, to stand on the border and separate the creature from the Creator. This same Word both pleads with the immortal as suppliant for afflicted mortality and acts as ambassador of the ruler to the subject. . . . [he is] neither uncreated as God, nor created as you, but midway between the two extremes, a surety to both sides" (*Heir* 42. 205-206). There is a bond of consubstantiality between him and the spiritual element of the human soul. The instrument of the creation, it is also through him that the soul effects its return to God: "For if we have not yet become fit to be thought sons of God yet we may be sons of His invisible image, the most holy Word" (*Con. Tongues* 28.147).

In such a system, whose framework, problems, and methods are those of Greek philosophy, there is hardly any place for narrowly nationalistic preoccupations. Messianic speculation plays only a secondary role in Philo's thought. Philo, of course, was writing for the pagans as well as the Jews, and thus it was not to his advantage to stress this point. But these considerations of expediency served only to reinforce a natural tendency of his temperament: Philo was not of an apocalyptic spirit.

Philo's thought, when compared with the major tendencies of Palestinian Judaism, might appear to be totally aberrant and truly heretical. In fact, judging from the complete silence of the Talmud in this respect, it would seem that Philo's coreligionists quickly lost all memory of him. But in his own time and place, far from being banished from the synagogue, Philo was its venerated spokesman. More than once he was entrusted with great responsibilities. In particular, to him was entrusted the very delicate task of pleading the cause of the Jews—in the face of Alexandrian anti-semitism—before the Emperor Caligula. If Philo was a heretic, then all of Alexandrian Judaism was heretical with him.

Moreover, despite very real differences, we should not conclude that there was a radical opposition between the diaspora and Palestine. Philo is quite representative of Alexandrian Judaism. He is less representative of the diaspora as a whole, which was undoubtedly split between the influence of Alexandria and that of Palestine. On the other hand, although the contrasts between Philo and the rabbis are immediately apparent, thére were also points of contact between them. Philo's Jewish consciousness was as lively as his admiration for the Israelite past. His observance of the law was above suspicion, even though it proceeded from different motives than that of Hillel or of Shammai, for example. Indeed, this latter point is the touchstone for judging the genuineness of his Judaism.

The doctrine of the Logos has biblical roots, specifically in the hypostasized Wisdom of the wisdom literature and, beyond these writings (themselves of a very Hellenistic spirit), in the concept of the Word of God at work in the universe. Of course, properly speaking, the rabbis knew nothing of divine hypostases. But the rabbinical concept of *memra* ("word") is an echo, no matter how weak and distorted, of the theory of powers. This is a type of thought and mysticism (somewhat analogous to that of Philo) which survived in the Kabbalah and in speculations on the ineffable Name and on the divine mode of action in the creation. Finally, to restrict ourselves to the chronological limits of this present study, some of the minor sects, as well as the Essenes themselves, present precise affinities with this aspect of Philo's thought. I can only mention this fact here, without developing it in detail.

At this time Pharisaism had not yet become Judaism, which was still flexible and many-sided. The marginal groupings were able to constitute a link between Pharisaism and Alexandrian theology, since these groups were open to the influence of both. This must be remembered if we wish to locate Philo in proper perspective. The fundamental differences between Philo and the rabbis of the Talmud undoubtedly explain how Philo was able to fall into total oblivion in Talmudic circles. But this oblivion should also be viewed as the aftereffect of the reaction of defense which, following the entrance of Christianity into the picture, led Judaism to become more inflexible and to cut itself off from Greek thought. The Pharisaic synagogue turned away from Philo because Christian theology found support in his thought, just as it had turned away from the Septuagint because it had become the official Bible of the church.

Therapeutae

It is also through Philo that we hear of the Jewish sect of the Therapeutae, to whom he devotes his treatise on the contemplative life. He is the only person to speak of this sect, and he does so in rather vague terms. Moreover, as was customary with Philo, he was obviously preoccupied with demonstrating to the Greeks that the Jews were their superiors in every thing, including the practice of philosophy. Thus we can wonder, with Father Lagrange, if Philo's description is not simply an "allegorical fiction of the great allegorist which expresses his ideal of Jewish life, studious and contemplative."

It is certainly difficult to separate reality from fiction in what Philo says. It is quite possible that the description which he gives, like that of the Palestinian sects (perhaps even more so), is exaggerated by his desire to accommodate to the Greek way of thinking both that of which he speaks and those whom he describes. However, it would be going too far to relegate the Therapeutae to the ranks of the mythical. When Philo states that they were found throughout the entire world, we have a right to be skeptical or at least to interpret what he says. Philosophical speculation and the way of life which it determines are not tied to any one place, any more than they are the exclusive privilege of one people. Philo knew the Greek thinkers too well to deny that they could have grasped the Divine and lived according to the rules of wisdom. In stating that the Therapeutae were everywhere, he was saying that throughout the world there are wise men worthy of admiration, whether they be disciples of Plato, of Pythagoras, or Brahmans. "For perfect goodness must needs be shared both by Greeks and the world outside Greece" (*Cont. Life* 3.21). But this is also to imply that, since all philosophy is in some way the tributary of the biblical revelation, the influence of the Bible is present everywhere. If then, at its limit, the term "Therapeutae" tends thus to include philosophers of every persuasion, it is nonetheless true that the perfect sage could only be a Jew nourished by Scripture and practicing its teaching. The true Therapeutae, thus called either because they engaged in spiritual healing or because they practiced a pure worship (*therapeia*) of the divinity, were disciples of Moses.

It is quite possible that Philo's description borrows certain traits from pagan conventicles of which he might have known (Pythagorean, for example). It could also represent, in certain respects, a sort of collective projection of what he himself wanted to be. Yet nothing gives us warrant to doubt that such a group of Jews, perhaps small in number, could have been found near Alexandria: animated by the same ideal that animated Philo, they would have attempted to live the perfect life, in community, according to methods borrowed from certain pagan schools of philosophy while yet basing their style of life on the Bible. It is not at all improbable that there was an Alexandrian Essenism. It would have been related to the Essenism of Palestine through the observance of the same religion and through a somewhat analogous rule; perhaps there were also explicit influences in one direction or the other. Yet Alexandrian Essenism would have been original in the sense that it was born in the milieu of Hellenism and was more receptive to the contribution of the Greek world.

Although we are much better informed concerning the Essenes, it is not difficult to draw out the points of contact and the differences between the two groups. Both were monastic-type communities, practicing an asceticism that was more severe among the Therapeutae than among the Essenes. Like the Essenes, the Therapeutae divested themselves of their possessions on entering the sect. Their "mother house" (if branches did indeed exist) was located on a hill near Lake Mareotis, in a place that was both secure and climatically healthy. The site was not dissimilar from that of Qumran. In both cases, cenobitic life was present alongside that of anchorite hermits. Just as the Essenes lived in huts and caves surrounding the monastery, so the Therapeutae inhabited individual cells (each with a private chapel or "inner chamber") in which they spent six days out of seven, leaving the cells only for the cultic gatherings on the sabbath. They ate a frugal meal, and only after sunset, and some of them went three and even six days without eating anything at all.

Whereas the Essenes led an active life, devoting almost the whole day to manual labor and reserving a part of the evening for study, the Therapeutae were devoted solely to pure contemplation. Every moment was taken up with solitary or collective study, meditation, and prayer: "The interval between early morning and evening is spent entirely in spiritual exercise" (*Cont. Life* 3.28). This is the basic difference between the two groups, which Philo emphasizes from the beginning of his treatise. It is nonetheless true that the properly religious exercises developed in Essenism according to forms that were clearly related to those practiced by the Therapeutae.

The Therapeutae, again like the Essenes, marked the rising and the setting of the sun by special prayers. Scripture nourished their meditation and their piety, since nothing was taken into their private chapels, whether "drink of food or any other of the things necessary for the needs of the body, but laws and oracles delivered through the mouth of prophets, and psalms and anything else which fosters and perfects knowledge and piety" (*Cont. Life* 3.25). What we have here, in short, are the various divisions of the biblical canon. But to these sacred books of Judaism were added a literature peculiar to the group, "writings of men of old, the founders of their way of thinking" (*Cont. Life* 3.29), as well as the hymns which successive generations of solitary men had continued to compose under the effect of divine inspiration. In this respect, one is reminded of the commentaries, apocalypses, and psalms of Qumran. The exegesis of the Therapeutae was of an allegorical type. Perhaps Philo was a bit too quick to emphasize in them what was a characteristic of his own exegesis. Yet since allegory was more or less a part of the spiritual patrimony of Alexandrian Judaism, it is not at all surprising that it had been indulged in, more precisely and more systematically than at Qumran, by a sect which was, undoubtedly, mainly of Alexandrian tradition and recruitment.

The Therapeutae differed from Qumran in that

they included women as well as men in their membership. The women, like the men, dedicated themselves to chastity. All gathered together for the sabbatical rites, grouped in a hierarchy according to age, with a partition separating the women from the men. The senior member, who by definition had the fullest knowledge of their doctrine and who also acted as president, gave a discourse. On the sabbath the diet was slightly less strict than during the week. But even on the seventh day, if we are to accept Philo's word, the meal was not elaborate, consisting of "common bread with salt for a relish flavoured further by the daintier with hyssop, and their drink is spring water" (*Cont. Life* 4.37).

A more solemn feast is celebrated "after seven sets of seven days," although we cannot tell if this involved a ceremony repeated every forty-nine days or, on the contrary, an annual rite. Perhaps both interpretations should be combined. Indeed, it is quite possible that this feast of weeks, regularly celebrated every seventh sabbath, was the occasion of a special celebration once a year. When Philo mentions in this regard "the eve of the chief feast which Fifty takes for its own, Fifty the most sacred of numbers" (*Cont. Life* 8.66), it is obvious that he is not thinking of any period of fifty days whatever, but of Pentecost. Apparently Pentecost was considered to be more solemn than the Passover itself, of which he makes no mention.

One notes here the importance attributed to the week as a unit of time. As we have seen, the same thing was true among the Essenes, who also sur-

rounded Pentecost with a special reverence, com-
memorating as it did the renewal of the covenant. It
was on Pentecost that they proceeded with the admission of new members. The similarity is undoubtedly
not fortuitous. There is good reason to suppose that
among the Therapeutae the annual celebration mark-
ing the eve of Pentecost also fell on a Saturday and
that consequently Pentecost itself was always celebrated on a Sunday, just as at Qumran. If this hypothesis could be proved, it would mean that the two
sects utilized the same calendar, which was different
from the official Jerusalem calendar. This would be
one more item in favor of a common origin of the two
sects. Moreover, it should be noted that the symbolism
of numbers, related to cosmological speculations,
occupied an important place among both Therapeutae
and Essenes. In fact, it seems to have played an even
greater role among the former than among the latter.
Philo explains the importance they attributed to the
number fifty as follows: "Fifty [is] the most sacred of
numbers and the most deeply rooted in nature, being
formed from the square of the right-angled triangle
which is the source from which the universe springs"
(*Cont. Life* 8.65). Such considerations were dear to
the Pythagoreans, for whom *penteconta* was a sacred
number par excellence. There is hardly any room for
doubt that the Therapeutae were influenced in a
direct fashion by the Pythagorean speculations.

The rites of the sect also reveal rather striking
similarities, on certain points, with the rites of Qumran. The Therapeutae, these exemplary ascetics who

without compromise rejected the pleasures of good food, still participated in a communal meal, celebrated perhaps every Saturday (Philo's testimony is not perfectly clear in this respect) and, in any event, on the feast of the forty-ninth day. This communal meal was the central act of their liturgy. Its importance is attested by the description Philo gives of it (*Cont. Life* 8.64-11.90).

After the initial prayer, the Therapeutae, dressed (like the Essenes) in white robes, would settle themselves at table, the men on the right and the women on the left. For the meal they reclined on couches that were "plank beds of the common kinds of wood, covered with quite cheap strewings of native papyrus" (*Cont. Life* 9.69). The president of the community, after general silence was established, would comment at length upon some passage from the Scriptures, doing so according to the allegorical method: "For to these people the whole law book seems to resemble a living creature with the literal ordinances for its body and for its soul the invisible mind laid up in its wording" (*Cont. Life* 10.78). Then the president would arise and sing a hymn, either newly composed or an old one by former members. Each member then would take turns singing, with the rest of the group remaining silent except for the refrains. Then the meal would follow, served by novices and consisting, like the meal of the sabbath day, of leavened bread (which was considered to be very pure because it played a role in the ritual of the temple), water, salt, and hyssop.

Next came the "sacred vigil." The refectory was

cleared of tables, and the group formed itself into two choirs, one of men and one of women. They would then begin to sing hymns, sometimes in unison, sometimes antiphonally, "hands and feet keeping time in accompaniment" (*Cont. Life* 11.84), thus imitating movements and maneuvers of a classical choir. Rapt with enthusiasm, and "having drunk as in the Bacchic rites of the strong wine of God's love," they finished by mixing together into a single choir like that formed after the crossing of the Red Sea, the men led by Moses and the women by Miriam. Thus they continued until morning prayer, which they recited standing and facing the east, their hands stretched toward the rising sun. Finally each returned to his private sanctuary.

There is no parallel to this curious liturgical dance in the Essene ritual nor, as far as we know, in any other Jewish circle of the period. This is not sufficient reason to contest its authenticity, even though Philo's description is not exempt from a certain affectation. The Qumran documents attest to the practice of antiphonal responses, spoken, chanted, or sung. Furthermore, the history of religions provides many examples of sacred dances. As far as Judaism is concerned, we need only consider David dancing before the Ark, or the Hasidim of eastern Europe in the eighteenth century. Generally speaking, "non-Westernized" Jews hold to the principle that the body should pray in unison with the soul and through its movements should keep time with the prayer of the heart and lips. This is what is expressed in the characteristic ritual swaying of certain synagogues. The dances of the Therapeutae represented an extreme example of this principle, influenced perhaps by the ecstatic manifestations of pagan religious rites. It is significant that in this context Philo alludes not only to the techniques of Greek theater but to Bacchic enthusiasm as well. Perhaps the comparison has more than a simply pedagogical and literary value.

It would be very interesting to know if the sacred meal had the same meaning for the Therapeutae that it had at Qumran, and if other rites analogous to those of the Essenes complemented it. Unfortunately Philo is silent on this point. Even concerning the meal, the similarity in the rite itself does not justify the conclusion that both groups understood it in the same manner. However, the affinities between the sects which we have pointed out seem to be quite real. They undoubtedly express a close relationship between the two sects, stemming perhaps from a common origin. On the other hand, it is clear that the group of Therapeutae owes its original traits, in large part, to the Alexandrian milieu in which it developed. The Therapeutae were to Essenism what Philo was to the rabbis of Palestine. Like Philo, the Therapeutae were preoccupied with ethics and cosmology, with allegory and mystical doctrines rather than with casuistry, nationalistic messianism, and eschatology. Like him, they conceived of the meditation and observance of the Torah, indeed, of their entire religion, in terms of wisdom. They illustrate, as does Philo, the accommodative faculties which characterized Judaism at the beginning of our era.

Eusebius, reading Philo through the eyes of a Christian of the fourth century, believed that he recognized in the Therapeutae the first representatives of Egyptian Christianity, standing in direct line with the monasticism of his own day (*Eccl. Hist.* 2.17.1 ff.). His view of things is naïve enough. Yet on this score Eusebius did at least indicate an awareness of a major question which is posed for us as we approach the end of this brief and rapid survey, namely, the question of the various connections that might have existed between the Jewish sects and the nascent church.

6

The Jewish Sects and Christianity

THE QUESTION of all the possible relations between the Jewish sects and Christianity is immense and difficult, and I cannot deal with it here in all its ramifications. However, it should at least be indicated briefly in what terms this question is posed and how one might go about seeking its solution.

First of all, it should be pointed out that Christianity, at the beginning, served only to add one more detail to a picture that was already singularly variegated. During the first stage of its development, Christianity constituted one Jewish sect among others. In Acts, "the sect [*hairesis*] of the Nazarenes" is mentioned (24:5) along with the "party [*hairesis*] of the Sadducees" (5:17) and the "party of the Pharisees" (15:5). This same alignment reappears in the work of the tenth-century Karaite author Jacob al-Kirkisani. In citing sources that undoubtedly reached back beyond his own time, Kirkisani mentions the Christians alongside the Pharisees, Sadducees, and Magharia ("people of the caves"), who apparently were the Essenes of

Qumran. But is it possible to discover a more direct, filial relationship between the nascent church and one or another of the Jewish groups that existed before the church came into being?

The ancient Christian writers were of definite opinions on this matter. Their opinion is formulated quite clearly by Justin Martyr, for example, and even better by Hegesippus, who presents the Jewish sects as the cradle of Christian heterodoxy. According to this account, a certain Thebouthis, "because he had not been made bishop, begins its [the church's] corruption by the seven heresies, to which he belonged, among the people" (Eusebius, *Eccl. Hist.* 4.22.4-5). From these seven sects, which are enumerated by the author, came "Simon, whence the Simonians," and a whole series of Christian heresiarchs (*ibid.*). It is hardly necessary to emphasize that this is a rather arbitrary view. It is evident that Hegesippus has schematized things and, furthermore, has confused the issue by transposing to the Judaism of the period before A.D. 70 a situation which really belonged to the Christianity of his own times, namely, a clearly drawn opposition between orthodoxy and heresy. When he surveys the various shades of Judaism, he does so by utilizing categories and structures that were familiar to him, that is, the Great Church on the one hand, the many forms of heterodoxy on the other. When he applied the term "heresies" to Jewish phenomena, he continued to utilize the term in its Christian sense, without taking account of the fact that it could not be applied with identical force and meaning to both religions. In such a perspective, Judaism evaporates, as it were, into thin air. It is no longer composed of anything but a congeries of mutally hostile heresies. No trace remains of the genuine religion of Israel, since Pharisaism itself is only one of these heresies, one aberration among several, and this before the appearance of Christianity. Moreover, since a sort of providential continuity exists in error as well as in truth, the Christian heresies are said to be derived from these Jewish heresies. In the same way, orthodox Christianity did not proceed from just any form of historic Judaism. No, it is seen as proceeding from that true religion as old as humanity itself, represented and practiced by Adam, Noah, the patriarchs, and the prophets. This true religion was unfolded in a continuous tradition throughout the course of biblical history; in the final analysis, it was already Christian.

For Hegesippus and for all the ancient church writers, orthodoxy (to speak only of Christianity) necessarily existed prior to all the forms of heresy (since orthodoxy was, in the final analysis, nothing other than the thought of Jesus itself). Consequently, this interaction between Jewish sects and Christianity, ending in the formation of Christian sects, could be only a phenomenon of the second hour: the truth is given first of all, and error is only a later distortion of it. Hegesippus, immediately before the passage relative to Thebouthis, says, "For this they called the church virgin, for it had not yet been corrupted by vain messages" (Eusebius, *op. cit.* 4.22.4-5).

Such a schema requires considerable retouching. For, although as we have seen, there is no doubt that some links and even sometimes a direct filiation did exist between certain marginal forms of Judaism and certain dissident Christian groups, it is equally certain that other supposedly heretical sects in ancient Christendom became such precisely because they remained fixed in archaic positions which had soon been abandoned by the church of the Gentiles. This was the case, for example, with Jewish-Christians of all shades, whose obstinate fidelity to Jewish law served only to perpetuate, on the fringes of orthodoxy, the attitude of the first Jerusalemite community. Contrary to what Hegesippus thought, it was actually the Great Church, following St. Paul, which played the role of innovator in relation to the position of these benighted Jewish-Christians. We now know that the relations between orthodoxy and heresy were much more complex at the beginnings of Christianity than Hegesippus realized.

On the other hand, we must concern ourselves with the important question of whether and how the first generation of Christianity, considered in its different expressions (as reflected, for example, in the writings of the New Testament), had been influenced by one or another of the Jewish sects.

It seems that we can ignore the two rival groups which constituted official Judaism at the time of Christ. Although the Book of Acts (6:7) informs us that many priests came to swell the ranks of the first faithful, it is clear that the Sadducean spirit and that of primitive Christianity diverged radically. The condemnation of Jesus had been instigated by the Sadducees, who were fundamentally hostile to any messianic surges. Although the church was given a sacerdotal structure somewhat analogous to that which was based on the temple, this was not a phenomenon of the first hour. It was born from a reading of the Old Testament, from which Christianity borrowed certain types and models, and not from any influence of the priestly party. It illustrates the deposition of former structures and the establishment, in their place, of the New Israel.

As far as the relations between Pharisaism and the teaching of Jesus are concerned, they have been amply studied.[1] Certain precise affinities existed, of course, but certain intractable oppositions were also present which prohibit us from seeking on this side the soil which nourished Christianity.[2] It appears certain that the Pharisees had not played the determining role in the trial of Jesus, yet nevertheless it was with a Judaism (after A.D. 70) identified with Pharisaism that Christianity consummated its break. The revolutionary preaching of St. Paul and the developments of Christology in a direction contrary to traditional monotheism had increasingly transformed the at least relative tolerance enjoyed by the nascent church in

---

[1] Cf., for example, I. Abrahams, *Studies in Pharisaism and the Gospels*, 2 vols. (Cambridge University Press, 1917 and 1924).

[2] On the nature of these oppositions, cf., among others, J. Parkes, *Judaism and Christianity* (Chicago: University of Chicago Press, 1948), pp. 57 ff., and H. J. Schoeps, "Jésus et la Loi juive," *RHPR*, 33 (1953), 1-20.

Israel into hostility and hatred. From that time on a rather intransigent orthodoxy began to develop and harden in rabbinical Judaism. This orthodoxy is typified in the famous Benediction (in this case a malediction) on the *minim* (heretics), which was introduced into the liturgy of the synagogue towards the end of the first century. This benediction was directed against all heretics, and in particular against the Christians,[3] who henceforth represented, in the Jewish point of view, a heresy in the current meaning of the term. Indeed, it was apparently the heresy par excellence. Jewish resistance toward Christianity was inspired by Pharisaism and organized around it. To be sure, Christianity at this time was no longer exactly identical, in its doctrinal affirmations, with the faith of the first disciples. But it is certain that the germ of the conflict with Pharisaism was already present in the initial stages of the church's development and in the preaching of Jesus.

Some scholars have thought it possible to discover a tie between nascent Christianity and the fanatic nationalists who were the Zealots. According to this thesis, which is connected with the name of Robert Eisler,[4] the initial Christian message would be that of

[3] [Such is the view of G. F. Moore, *Judaism in the First Centuries of the Christian Era*, vol. 1 (Cambridge, Mass.: Harvard University Press, 1927) , p. 91. I. Abrahams, *A Companion to the Authorized Daily Prayer Book* (3rd ed.; London: Eyre and Spottiswoode, 1932) , pp. lxiv f., denies that the Christians were the object of this curse. The Benediction in question is: "Let the Nazarenes and the heretics perish as in a moment, let them be blotted out of the book of the living and let them not be written with the righteous" (quoted in W. Foerster, *From the Exile to Christ*, trans. Gordon E. Harris [Philadelphia: Fortress Press, 1964], p. 157) .]

[4] [Cf., for example, R. Eisler, *The Messiah Jesus and John the Baptist* (New York: Dial Press 1931) .]

a political messianism, aiming to install the kingdom of Jesus, by force if need be, in a Palestine swept clean of Romans and of all idolatries. This same idea has been taken up once again, recently, in a more qualified and less systematic form, by S. G. F. Brandon.[5] This author tries to explain the total eclipse of the second-generation Jerusalem church by the fact that its leaders and members were directly and actively involved in the revolt of 66-70. The fall of the Holy City thus would have dealt the Jerusalem church such a hard blow that it never recovered from it. Brandon's thesis requires an impugning of Hegesippus' claim that at the beginning of hostilities the apostolic community migrated from Jerusalem to Pella. On the other hand, his thesis necessitates the acceptance of those extremely suspect passages from a Slavonic version of Josephus upon which Eisler had previously erected his whole theory. This is the weakness in Brandon's thesis, as it was with that of his predecessor.

It is not difficult to give an explanation for the rapid obscurity into which the Jerusalem church fell. For one thing, it was isolated, at least temporarily, from the rest of Christendom; moreover, it had remained attached to the norms of Jewish ritualism. Such considerations render superfluous the hypothesis of an active participation in the war, at least as a body. Of course, some of its members could have been seized by the nationalistic fever and, thinking that the events were the prelude to their Master's return in

---

[5] S. G. F. Brandon, *The Fall of Jerusalem and the Christian Church* (2nd ed.; London: S.P.C.K., 1957).

glory, could have given a helping hand to the insurgents. Even among Jesus' disciples was one named Simon the Zealot. But the Gospels designate him as such apparently because he was an exception. Furthermore, there is reason to believe that he broke with his former allegiance when he threw his lot in with Jesus. It is also a possibility that other disciples were in similar situations, beginning with Peter. In any case, it is certain that the milieu in which Jesus lived and acted was saturated with the Zealot spirit. Jesus himself, put to death by the Romans as a Zealot, constantly had to make clear his position over against this militant wing of Jewish nationalism.[6] He disavowed this movement, being no more attached to it than he was to Pharisaism.

Alexandrian Influences

In effect, it is in regard to the marginal sects, on the one hand, and Alexandrian Judaism, on the other, that the question is raised of a possible influence on nascent Christianity. From the first generation, certain elements in the church, in interpreting the Bible, had made use of the allegorism dear to the Alexandrians. The filiation here is beyond all doubt. But the method in the hands of the Christians was distinctive in two ways as compared with its use by Philo or by the *Letter of Aristeas*. The interpretation of the prescriptions of ritual law no longer involved

---

[6] O. Cullmann, *The State in the New Testament* (New York: Charles Scribner's Sons, 1956), pp. 12 ff.

conferring on them an additional authority. Quite the contrary, the Christian method involved showing that these prescriptions had *only* symbolic value. Perhaps at the start it had been legitimate to take them literally, but this was no longer the case since the coming of Christ and the inauguration of the new covenant.

The second distinctive element in this method follows on the first. The Christians did not cease to seek the expression of metaphysical or ethical truths in the biblical precepts and stories (the *Epistle of Barnabas* does this abundantly, along the lines of the *Letter of Aristeas*). However, and more frequently, they also saw in these narratives and precepts the veiled announcement of Gospel events and of ecclesiastical rites and institutions. The contradistinction is no longer solely between two worlds, that of appearance and that of reality; it is also, and above all, between two successive phases of the religious history of humanity, that of the promises and that of the fulfillment. For the Letter to the Hebrews, the ritual law is both "a copy and shadow of the heavenly" (8:5, NEB) and also "a shadow ... of the good things which were to come" (10:1, NEB). The historical perspectives became diluted in Philo's thought. Christian thought restored them in all their force, and allegory was changed into typology: the sacrifice of Isaac presages that of Christ, the crossing of the Jordan prefigures baptism. Thus a method borrowed from the Jews is turned against them. But no one contests the reality of the borrowing.

This borrowing, moreover, was not limited to the

exegetical method. There are numerous affinities between Philo and certain of the New Testament writings. Philo undoubtedly was dependent on a tradition of thought going back to the Septuagint, a tradition whose properly theological aspects are fixed in the book the Wisdom of Solomon. It is in this corner that we must seek the source common to Philo and the New Testament. Whereas in Philo's work it is often difficult to distinguish between that which he owes to his predecessors and that which represents his personal contributions, the same cannot be said, in certain cases, for the writings of the New Testament. There are some cases where the similarities are too clear, both in vocabulary and in ideas, for us to exclude the hypothesis of a direct influence of Philo's writings on the authors of the New Testament.

It is improbable that there was any such influence on St. Paul, who was Philo's immediate contemporary and who undoubtedly did not have occasion to read him. The distinction between the heavenly man and the earthly man, which appears in both, represents one of the themes of a certain form of Jewish speculation of the time. Moreover, St. Paul gives it a quite different interpretation from that of Philo, since for the one the earthly man is chronologically first, while for the other the heavenly man comes first.

On the other hand, the prologue of the Fourth Gospel and its Logos doctrine offer parallels of thought and expression with Philo which are so precise that it is difficult to explain them without presupposing certain borrowings or reminiscences. However, although the literary dependence is scarcely to be doubted, it cannot hide the fundamentally different meaning attached to the two doctrines. A number of traits and attributes of Philo's Logos reappear in the Johannine Logos, often expressed in identical terms. But whereas Philo's Logos, although embracing the entire universe, remains close to God and without any contact with matter, the Johannine Logos "became flesh," an unthinkable assertion for Philonic theology. The whole system of Johannine thought is conditioned by the person of Christ, in whom merge the level of transcendence and that of history.

Philo had already tended sometimes to identify the Logos with the heavenly man whom I have just mentioned. In the Fourth Gospel this identification is clearly made. But it is made in relation to the earthly Christ, the incarnate Logos, who is also the Son of man who came down from heaven (John 3:13). At the same time, there is another identification which would never have been made either by Philo, who was little concerned with messianism and eschatology, or by the Palestinians, who were little inclined to hypostatic speculation. This was the identification of the Logos with the Messiah. Theologically, this is the fundamental distinctiveness of Christianity in relation to Judaism. But would Christianity ever have come to explain Jesus in terms of Logos if the word and the concept had not been popularized by Philo?

Things are even clearer when it comes to the Letter to the Hebrews, whose "Philonism" has long impressed exegetes. This has been shown with all the clarity one could desire by C. Spicq, one of the most recent commentators on the subject. I can only refer the reader to Spicq's detailed and searching analyses.[7] To cite the most important points, and without mentioning the numerous and remarkable similarities of vocabularly, we find analogies in the relationship between the Son-Logos and the Father, in the Jewish cult on earth and the heavenly cult, and in the function of the High Priest (assumed by the Philonic Logos on the one hand, by Christ on the other). These analogies are too striking to be fortuitous. One can conclude, with Spicq, that the author of the Letter to the Hebrews "was not ignorant of the works of Philo" and indeed was "a Philonian converted to Christianity."

In the light of these brief examples, we can better understand why Judaism, which had elaborated and utilized the Philonic method primarily for apologetic and missionary ends, started to turn away from it when the Christians turned it to their own account. The total disappearance of the Alexandrian type of Judaism came shortly after the church entered the picture. There is a certain causal relationship between these two facts. The church welcomed the spirit and undoubtedly also the clientele of the Hellenistic synagogue.

However real was the influence of Philo and of his

---

[7] C. Spicq, "Le philonisme de l'Epitre aux Hébreux," *RB*, 56 (1949), 542 ff. and 57 (1950), 218 ff. See also the same author's substantial commentary on Hebrews in the series "Études bibliques" (Paris, 1954). [In English see S. G. Sowers, *The Hermeneutics of Philo and Hebrews* (Richmond: John Knox, 1965).]

categories of thought on nascent Christianity, only the specifically theological aspect of Christianity was affected. This influence was especially clear in the area of Christology. The Christians transposed and adapted Philonic themes in order to explain the person and role of their Master. Thus it was, in the history of Christian origins, a phenomenon of the second hour. If contact was to be established with Jewish-Hellenistic thought, the gospel had to be carried outside of the Galilean and Jerusalem environment where it had first been preached. Before making use of the Philonic doctrine of the Logos, the first Christians had thought of Jesus in terms that were more specifically biblical: prophet, messiah, Son of man, suffering servant. Although influences from Alexandrian-Judaism contributed greatly to the shaping of Christian theology, they played no part in the genesis of Christianity itself. The terrain where Christianity was born and which nourished it must be sought in Palestine.

Palestinian Influences

Christianity represented, in the midst of the Judaism of the age, an original movement. Yet it was informed by a certain context. Scholars of all persuasions are now agreed on this. Only a few extremists, prompted by more or less conscious polemical or apologetical preoccupations, refuse to see in Christianity anything but a simple by-product of Jewish or Hellenistic religiousness or, on the contrary, in the name of Christianity's absolute transcendence, repudiate the sacrilegious idea that it could in any way bear the marks of the environment in which it originated. No historical phenomenon develops in isolation, and Christianity is no exception. Although there is scarcely any doubt regarding the reality of the influences which shaped it, the whole question is one of appreciating these in their proper measure.

The problem is posed in all its sharpness in regard to the Dead Sea scrolls. It is reassuring to the historian to be able to state that the many initial differences of scholarly opinion have been slowly but surely reduced, and that a moderate view is steadily gaining ground. Scholars are almost unanimous in recognizing that the Qumran documents throw a new light on Christian origins. They differ only on the extent of the influences, their import, and their precise course.

The role played by John the Baptist in the beginnings of Jesus' preaching is solidly attested. There is fairly general agreement that the baptism of John, which Jesus himself received, was the point of origin of Christian baptism. John the Baptist preached a message that is not dissimilar to that of the Essenes, and he did so on the banks of the Jordan, only a few miles to the north of Qumran. One cannot assert, of course, that he had belonged to the Qumran community before gathering an autonomous sect around himself. Yet he must at least have been in contact with this group and have known its characteristics. Moreover, it should be noted that John the Baptist, who also came from priestly circles, represented that same reformist tendency from which the dissidence of the Essenes was born. Under these circumstances, it is normal to seek in the Baptist the link (or one of the links) between Essenism and Christianity.

Perhaps there were even more direct contacts. Essenism presents precise similarities with various branches of the primitive church, in particular with the Hellenists and, even more clearly, with the Jewish-Christian Ebionites. The strict legalism of the Ebionites, coupled nevertheless with a violent hostility toward the temple and sacrificial worship and with a dualistic system of thought, reminds one of the position of the Qumran sectarians. Perhaps we are dealing here with movements which were initially independent of each other though somehow related. But since Essenism disappeared from the scene at the same time that Christianity entered it, there is every reason to believe that Essenism provided Christianity with some of it recruitment, starting at the very beginning and perhaps increasing after A.D. 70. It is not impossible that some of Christ's immediate disciples had come from Essenism. Some have even supposed, without being able to bring forth any proof, that Jesus himself had been a member of the sect. The hypothesis has little basis. Jesus' ministry, in its essentials, unfolds in Galilee, and there is nothing to indicate that he had spent a prolonged period in the Judean wilderness before receiving the baptism of John. For even more cogent reasons it is impossible to identify Jesus with the Teacher of Righteousness of the Essene writings.

To be sure, the two occupy quite similar places in the movements each inspired, and in the veneration of their followers. The Essenes seem to have recognized in their Teacher the emulator and probably the equal of Moses. Indeed, the mystery surrounding his name, ineffable perhaps like that of God, could permit us to suppose that they placed him even higher than Moses. The Thanksgiving Hymns, which are apparently in part the work of the Teacher, apply prophetic passages to him. This is true, in particular, of the passages in Isaiah relative to the suffering servant (for example, chap. 53), which Jesus also applied to himself and which the first Christians applied to him. There are remarkable similarities between the fate of Christ and that of the Teacher of Righteousness, who was followed by a few disciples, scoffed at by the masses, persecuted and perhaps put to death by the official priesthood, and exalted by God because of his sufferings. Like Christ, he had an acute awareness of his vocation, and expressed it in terms which more than once presage the terminology of the New Testament. God revealed all mysteries to him, and he in turn communicated to his disciples the fullness of his knowledge. Thus he was the agent of divine revelation and, consequently, the instrument of salvation. Some passages in the Hymns even suggest the outline of an ecclesiology. For example, the Teacher declares:

And [Thou] has established my fabric upon rock;
and everlasting foundations serve me for my ground
and all my walls are a tried rampart
which nothing can shake.

—Thanksgiving Hymns, VII, 8-9

This building could be, metaphorically, the very person—physical and moral—of the Teacher. But it could also be the community of his disciples, of which he is the cornerstone as it were, the rock of "those who had entered my Covenant" (V, 23). It is hardly necessary to emphasize the very Christian sound which such passages have. Just as the primitive church proclaimed the advent of a new covenant, sealed by the blood of Christ (1 Cor. 11:25), and titled its holy book the New Covenant (a more exact translation than the New Testament), so also the Qumran sect in certain of its writings calls itself the community of the new covenant. It is as though the church, concerned to portray its Master and to clarify its own self-understanding, had borrowed from the Essenes a repertory of terms and concepts, a certain number of theological schemata, and perhaps also collections of biblical verses, chosen and grouped in accordance with apologetical and catechetical ends. Indeed, the literature of the *Testimonia* was already represented at Qumran before being appropriated by and developed in primitive Christianity.

But these similarities, no matter how striking, should not make us forget the equally clear differences. It seems indeed that the Essenes, like the Christians, had awaited their Teacher's return in glory and, in some way, had associated him with the inauguration of the coming kingdom. Yet it is not quite certain that they had identified him with one of the two messiahs whom they expected. Moreover, although it is possible that the Teacher of Righteousness died a martyr, nothing justifies our assuming that his disciples attached a soteriological and redemptive meaning to his passion, nor that they taught his resurrection.

If we consider only the earthly careers of the Teacher of Righteousness and of Christ, obvious differences appear. The former was a priest, coming from the Jerusalem priesthood; an exacting ascetic, he communicated a secret and exclusive teaching to a closed group of disciples. The latter was a Galilean of humble extraction, who preached his message in the byways of Palestine, more concerned with reaching the sinful masses than with isolating himself from them. The one outdid the law, multiplying its observances. The other interpreted the Mosaic commandment, sometimes reinforcing it but also sometimes making it more pliable and even abrogating it; in any case, he manifested an authority equal or superior to that of the law. It would be easy, but superfluous, to press the parallelism between them. It appears certain that Jesus knew Essenism, or an environment in which Essenian beliefs were particularly widespread. It is also certain that when his disciples attempted to interpret his person, their theological reflection found certain guidelines among Essenian precedents. But however real these influences, they were not passively experienced and do not permit us to conclude a pure and simple filiation.

On the contrary, certain aspects of Jesus' preaching seem to betray a deliberate preoccupation with defining himself over against Essenism. Thus when he proclaimed that the first shall be last, when he prescribed that one should not judge in order not to be judged, when he placed the "wise" and the "understanding" over against children to whom God has confided his secrets, it could be that this was a barely concealed polemic addressed to Essenism, to its hierarchy, its judicial system, its scorn of the "simple." And when the Lucan parable (14:21) conveys "the poor and maimed and blind and lame" to the messianic banquet, one naturally thinks of the regulation of Qumran which excluded from the sect "every person smitten in his flesh, paralysed in his feet or hands, lame or blind or deaf or smitten in his flesh with a blemish visible to the eye" (Society Manual Annex 2:5-7). There is a total opposition on all these points, which Dupont-Sommer quite rightly emphasizes.[8]

Moreover, it should not be forgotten that official Judaism, whether Pharisaic or Sadducean, also conceived of society in hierarchal form and regulated by an extensive judiciary apparatus. The scorn of the "simple folk" was common to the Essenes and the Pharisees, and the interdictions formulated by the Qumran rule relative to the physically unsound are an echo of similar prohibitions in regard to the priesthood (Lev. 21:17 ff.). However hostile the Essenes might have been to the people of Jerusalem, in this case they were on the side of the Jerusalemites. They were not on the side of Christ, who in this instance condemned not only the Qumran sect but the whole of Judaism in some of its fundamental norms.

---

[8] Dupont-Sommer, *The Essene Writings*, pp. 375 ff.

Qumran and Primitive Christianity

Seeing these contrasts should serve to make us more cautious regarding the affinities. We should not lose sight of the fact that certain traits identical or analogous in both the primitive church and at Qumran belonged also to what could be called the common Judaism of the epoch. For example, eschatological beliefs and the expectation of the end of time are present, with more or less precision and force, in many sectors of Jewish thought at the beginning of our era. Moreover, at least a part of the originally esoteric literature represented at Qumran, and probably developed to a great extent by the sect itself, quickly came into the public domain and contributed to the diffusion beyond Qumran and its branches of a more or less distorted and sometimes insipid form of Essenian ideology. A direct influence can be concluded between Essenism and the primitive church only if attention is called to truly distinctive and specific elements characterizing these two groups and them alone.

In this respect, it should be noted that certain Jewish ideas or beliefs stood out in especially bold relief at Qumran and among the first Christians because they were in some way connected with the person of the Teacher of Righteousness or of Christ. This is the case, as we have seen, with the concept of the congregation of the elect (the "remnant" of Israel). The same is true of ideas relative to the kingdom, which is anticipated in some manner by the holy community and in which the Teacher seems called upon to play a role (albeit in a less precise fashion than Christ). Both the Essene sect and the church of Jerusalem, living in the expectation of the final events, organized themselves in collectivist structures and practiced the community of goods. But the break with official Judaism appears to have been more radical in the case of the Essenes, isolated in the wilderness, than in the case of the first followers of Jesus. The rites of Qumran were clearly substituted for those of the one sanctuary in Jerusalem. The rites of the Christians, "attending the temple together and breaking bread in their homes" (Acts 2:46), were initially only added to those of the temple.

It is still an open question whether or not Jesus celebrated the Last Supper according to the Essenian calendar. If he did, this would explain the contradiction between the Synoptics, which make it a Passover meal, and the Fourth Gospel, which denies it the character of a Passover meal. This would also create one more link, and a narrow one, between the two groups.[9] At least there was a precise formal analogy between the Christian Eucharist and the Essenian liturgy. The blessing of the bread and wine constituted, of course, one of the elements of Jewish domestic worship as it already seems to have been practiced in the time of Christ. Thus the relationship

---

[9] Cf. on this point, A. Jaubert, *The Date of the Last Supper*, trans. Isaac Rafferty (Staten Island, N.Y.: Alba House, 1965). [For further discussion of this point, see J. A. Walther, "The Chronology of Passion Week," *JBL*, 77 (1958), 116-122; G. Ogg's review of Jaubert, *La date de la cène*, in *NT*, (1959), 317-320; A. Jaubert, "Jésus et la calendrier de Qumran," *NTS*, 7 (1960), 1-30; M. H. Shepherd, Jr., "Are Both the Synoptics and John Correct about the Date of Jesus' Death?" *JBL*, 80 (1961), 123-132; Eugen Ruckstuhl, *Chronology of the Last Days of Jesus*, trans. Victor J. Drapela (New York: Desclée, 1965).]

between Essenism and Christianity in this matter does not involve the rite itself but rather the particular meaning which was given to it. At Qumran as well as among the first Christians, the blessing of the bread and wine is conceived of as an anticipation of the eschatological banquet which will group the righteous about the Messiah (or, in Essenism, the two Messiahs). As I have tried to show previously, the meal, at Qumran as in the church, is a sacramental rite and not simply a communal meal, for the non-initiated cannot participate in it. The parallel appears in a clearer light when we recall that in the practice of the primitive church, the Eucharist was normally celebrated on the occasion of the agape, the fraternal meal. Moreover, it is possible that the Essenes had conferred some sort of sacrificial meaning on their communal meal, since they abstained from the sacrifices of the temple. On the other hand, we are not justified in thinking that they had related the elements to the body and blood of their Teacher, for we are not absolutely certain that he had died a violent death. Once again, incontestable similarities are coupled with differences that are equally striking.

Furthermore, these differences are more or less distinct, and bear on quite diverse areas, according to which faction of the early church we consider. For the church was far from constituting a uniform bloc. As in the Judaism of the period, everything was in flux. Many diverse currents met in the church, intermingled, and sometimes came into conflict. Although the Jewish-Christian Ebionites may seem to be, in certain respects, the spiritual offspring of the Essenes, it is surely remarkable that the opposite wing of nascent Christianity also seems to have received the imprint of Essenism. Indeed, Essenism already seems to have presented the rough outlines of a doctrine of justification by faith, such as St. Paul was to introduce into the heart of the Christian message. The Predictions of Habakkuk states, "God will deliver [the Righteous] from the House of Judgment because of their affliction and their faith in the Teacher of Righteousness" (8:2). But the document does not set this faith in opposition to works of the law, which are, on the contrary, observed with an exemplary zeal. Likewise, there is nothing here equivalent to the christocentric mysticism of the apostle. In the same way, the opposition between light and darkness is a theme common to the Qumran scrolls and the Fourth Gospel, which, of all the New Testament writings, offers perhaps the most precise affinities with Essenism in its theological thought as well as in its phraseology. One reason the scrolls are significant is that they pose the Johannine question in new terms and bring to the question valuable elements for a solution.

The list of analogies could be lengthened considerably. These few examples will suffice, I think, to show that they are both too general or too indefinite in many respects for one to be able to conclude that there was a direct line of filiation (moreover, the differences must be taken into account) but also that at a number of points they are too precise to be purely fortuitous. Obviously, Essenism does not provide a solution for all the problems raised by the history of Christian origins. Although we can discover Essenism's imprint, of varying depth, in all the sectors of primitive Christianity, does this mean that Jesus, the twelve, James the brother of the Lord, Paul, Stephen, John, the Jewish-Christians, and the Hellenists all passed through the monastery of Qumran? To pose the question is to answer it: the hypothesis is absurd. Any one of the protagonists of Christian history could initially have been in direct contact with the recluses of the Judean wilderness. But if they all seem to owe something to the Essenes, it is because Essenism, diffused by its branches or by its writings, had affected to a certain degree all those in Israel who were not strictly of Sadducean or Pharisaic persuasion. In fact, it is not impossible that it had penetrated even into the ranks of the Pharisees. It could have reached primitive Christianity by many and diverse means.

Perhaps the picture would be modified if we knew better the other Jewish sects of the periphery. But it is unlikely that it would be fundamentally different. For, in any event, Essenism, as it has been reconstructed in all its particulars, constituted one of the major and probably the most important constituents of this marginal Judaism. It is not by chance that Josephus, excluding all other groups, described it alongside the two official parties. At the same time that they illustrate the complexity of Jewish life at the time, the Qumran scrolls also throw a new and invaluable light on the background out of which nascent Christianity arose.

Glossary

APOCRYPHA

From the Greek adjective meaning "hidden"; refers to a collection of works (usually numbered at fourteen or fifteen) which were rejected from the Hebrew canon but included in the Septuagint (*q.v.*) and Latin Vulgate.

ARAMAIC

A Semitic language used in the ancient Near East and presumed to be the language spoken by Jesus; a few Aramaic passages are found in the Old Testament.

BACCHIC

Of or pertaining to Bacchus, the Hellenistic-Roman god of wine.

BAR COCHBA

The leader of the second Jewish revolt against Rome (A.D. 132-135), who was hailed by Rabbi Akiba as the expected Jewish Messiah.

BENE ZADOK

"Sons of Zadok," that is, of the Zadokite (therefore priestly) line; the term is used in connection with both Essenes and Sadducees.

EPISTLE OF BARNABAS

An early Christian work by an unknown author which contains a strong attack on Judaism and claims that the Old Testament, rightly interpreted, provides testimonies (see *Testimonia*) to Christ and the church.

GOYIM

Literally, "the nations"; a rabbinic term signifying the Gentiles.

HABUROTH

Religious fellowships, whose precise nature and purpose are disputed. It has been suggested that Jesus and the twelve formed such a *haburah*.

HASIDEANS

The Greek form of the Hebrew *Hasidim* (*q.v.*); found, e.g., in 1 Macc. 2:42.

HASIDIM

Literally, the "pious" or "godly"; a party of conservative Jews who joined the Maccabean revolt against Antiochus Epiphanes (168 B.C.), but withdrew from the movement for national independence once religious liberty had been achieved (162 B.C.).

HASMONEANS

The family name of the Maccabees (*q.v.*).

KABBALAH

A term designating Jewish esoteric lore.

KARAITES

A Jewish sect originating in the eighth century A.D. and continuing down to the present which claims to follow the written

Torah and rejects the oral tradition of rabbinical Judaism.

KIRKISANI, JACOB AL-
Or, Yaqub al-Qirqisani; an Iraqi Karaite (*q.v.*) scholar of the tenth century A.D.

KITTIM
In the book of Genesis (10:4) one of the sons of Javan whose descendants settled on Cyprus; the name seems to have come to be applied to the coastlands of the eastern Mediterranean, and as used in the Dead Sea scrolls probably refers to Rome (cf. Dan. 11:30).

LETTER OF ARISTEAS
A Jewish pseudepigraphical (*q.v.*) work in Greek which describes how the Septuagint (*q.v.*) came to be miraculously written.

LEVITES
Israelite cultic officials whose functions and exact relation to the priests is disputed. The name is derived from "Levi," the third son of Jacob and Leah (Gen. 29:34).

MACCABEES
The family and followers of Judas ben Mattathias, called "Maccabeus" ("the Mallet-headed"?); they led the fight to free Judea from the Syrian yoke in the first part of the second century B.C.

MAIMONIDES
A Jewish philosopher (A.D. 1135-1204) who attempted to achieve a synthesis of the biblical revelation and Aristotelian philosophy; he is noted for his work *Guide for the Perplexed* and for the Thirteen Principles (*q.v.*).

MANDAEANS
A Semitic, gnostic sect which emerged in the early centuries of the Christian era and still exists in Iraq and Iran; John the Baptist plays a principal role in some writings of the sect.

MAZDAISM
See Zoroastrianism.

MEMRA
Literally, "word"; a term used in late Judaism to signify God in his expression and action.

MINYAN
"Portion"; the minimum number (fixed at ten) of Jewish male adults required to constitute a synagogue.

MISHNAH
Literally, "instruction"; the authoritative collection of Jewish oral law which forms

	the basis for the Talmud $(q.v.)$; its com-pilation is usually attributed to Judah ha-Nasi *ca.* A.D. 200.
NAZIRITES	Or "Nazarites"; a group of Israelites who consecrated themselves to the service of God and vowed to abstain from eating or drinking the produce of the vine, to leave their hair uncut, and to avoid contact with dead bodies (Num., chap. 6); the vow was for a limited period only.
PSEUDEPIGRAPHA	Jewish writings not included in either the Old Testament or the Apocrypha $(q.v.)$; some of the works were ascribed to famous figures with a view to enhancing the authority of the writings.
RECHABITES	A Jewish family group (from Jehonadab, son of Rechab, 2 Kings, chap. 10) which protested against the settled, agricultural life of Canaanite society and called for a return to the nomadic style of life of the Wilderness period. See Jer., chap. 35.
RELIGIO LICITA	Literally, "lawful religion"; refers to the Roman process of registration and authorization by which a religion became a "tolerated cult" in the eyes of the law.
SELEUCID	The dynasty founded by Seleucus, one of Alexander's generals; the Seleucid kings ruled from Syria for two and a half centuries, up to the period of Roman hegemony.
SEPTUAGINT	The Greek translation of the first five books of the Bible, made in Alexandria in the third century B.C.; as translations of other Old Testament books (including apocryphal writings) were produced, they were added to the others and the whole came to be known as the Septuagint.
SHEOL OF ABADDON	*Sheol* is used in the Old Testament gen-erally to refer to the place of the dead; *abaddon* ("destruction") is perhaps a synonym of Sheol or refers to a level of punishment within Sheol.
TALMUD	The great corpus of Jewish religious learn-ing consisting of the Mishnah $(q.v.)$ and

the Gemara, or exegesis and interpretation of the Mishnah; two versions of the Talmud were completed, the Palestinian Talmud in the fifth century A.D., the Babylonian Talmud a century later.

TESTIMONIA

Certain passages of the Old Testament used by the early church, according to some scholars, as "testimonies" to Christ.

TETRAGRAMMATON

Literally, "four letters"; the ineffable Name YHWH.

THIRTEEN PRINCIPLES

The articles of faith formulated by Maimonides (q.v.) which are commonly accepted as representing the nearest approach to a Jewish creed.

YAHWISM

The religion of the Israelites, from the ineffable Name YHWH.

ZOROASTRIANISM

An Iranian religion based on the teachings of Zoroaster (Zarathustra); its beliefs and doctrines centered about the chief cosmic deity Ahura Mazda.

Selected Bibliography

Ancient Sources

Apocrypha, The. Revised Standard Version. New York: Thomas Nelson & Sons, 1957.

EUSEBIUS. *The Ecclesiastical History.* Translated by K. Lake and J. E. L. Oulton. (Loeb Classical Library.) Vol. 1, London: William Heinemann, and New York: G. P. Putnam's Sons, 1926. Vol. 2, London: William Heinemann, and Cambridge, Mass.: Harvard University Press, 1932.

JOSEPHUS, FLAVIUS. *Works.* Translated by H. St. J. Thackeray, R. Marcus, A. Wikgren, and L. H. Feldman. (Loeb Classical Library.) 9 vols. London: William Heinemann, and Cambridge, Mass.: Harvard University Press, 1926-65.

JUSTIN MARTYR. *Writings of Saint Justin Martyr.* Translated by T. B. Falls. ("Fathers of the Church.") New York: Christian Heritage, 1948.

———. *Selections from Justin Martyr's Dialogue with Trypho, a Jew.* Translated and edited by R. P. C. Hanson. ("World Christian Books," No. 49.) New York: Association Press, 1964.

Mishnah, The. Translated, with Introduction and Notes, by Herbert Danby. London: Oxford University Press, 1933 (reprinted from corrected sheets of the first edition, 1964).

PHILO OF ALEXANDRIA. *Works.* Translated by F. H. Colson, G. H. Whitaker, and R. Marcus. (Loeb Classical Library.) 12 vols. London: William Heinemann, New York: G. P. Putnam's Sons, and Cambridge, Mass.: Harvard University Press, 1929-53.

PLINY. *Natural History.* Translated by H. Rackham and W. H. S. Jones. (Loeb Classical Library.) 10 vols. London: William Heinemann, and Cambridge, Mass.: Harvard University Press, 1938-46.

General Works on Judaism and the Major Sects

BONSIRVEN, J. *Palestinian Judaism in the Time of Jesus Christ.* Translated by William Wolf. New York: McGraw-Hill, 1965.

FOERSTER, W. *From the Exile to Christ: A Historical Introduction to Palestinian Judaism.* Translated by Gordon E. Harris. Philadelphia: Fortress Press, 1964.

GUIGNEBERT, C. *The Jewish World in the Time of Jesus.* Translated by S. H. Hooke, New York: Alfred A. Knopf, 1935.

LAGRANGE, M. J. *Le judaïsme avant Jésus-Christ.* Paris, 1931.

LIGHTLEY, J. W. *Jewish Sects and Parties in the Time of Jesus.* London: Epworth, 1925.

MOORE, G. F. *Judaism in the First Centuries of the Christian Era.* 3 vols. Cambridge, Mass.: Harvard University Press, 1927-30.

ROWLEY, H. H. *The Relevance of Apocalyptic.* 3rd ed., rev. and enlarged; New York: Association Press, 1964.

RUSSELL, D. S. *The Method and Message of Jewish Apocalyptic.* ("Old Testament Library.") Philadelphia: Westminster Press and London: SCM Press, 1964. For further titles on intertestamental and extrabiblical subjects, see the excellent bibliography, pp. 406-430.

SCHÜRER, E. *A History of the Jewish People in the Time of Jesus Christ.* Translated by J. Macpherson, S. Taylor, and P. Christie. Edinburgh: T. & T. Clark, 1886-90. An abridgement of the First Division of this work, edited and introduced by Nahum N. Glatzer, has been published in paperback edition. New York: Schocken, 1961.

Sadducees

LESZINSKY, R. *Die Sadduzäer.* Berlin, 1912.
(See also *infra,* "Pharisees," and *supra,* "General Works. . . .")

Pharisees

DAVIES, W. D. *Introduction to Pharisaism.* ("Facet Books—Biblical Series," No. 16.) Philadelphia: Fortress Press, 1967.

FINKELSTEIN, L. *The Pharisees.* 2 vols. Philadelphia: Jewish Publication Society of America, 1938 (3rd ed., 1963)

HERFORD, R. T. *Pharisaism, Its Aim and Its Method.* New York: G. P. Putnam's Sons, 1912.

———. *The Pharisees.* New York: Macmillan, 1924.

Zealots

FARMER, W. R. *Maccabees, Zealots, and Josephus.* New York: Columbia University Press, 1956.

Essenes

For a more extensive bibliography on the Essenes, see *M.* BURROWS, *The Dead Sea Scrolls* and *More Light on the Dead Sea Scrolls* (up through 1957) and, less extensive but more recent, H. RINGGREN, *The Faith of Qumran.* The following titles are intended simply as an introduction to the literature on the Essenes, which has now reached literally into the thousands of articles, monographs, and books.

BROWNLEE, W. H. *The Meaning of the Qumran Scrolls for the Bible, with Special Attention to the Book of Isaiah.* New York: Oxford University Press, 1964.

BRUCE, F. F. *Biblical Exegesis in the Qumran Texts.* Grand Rapids: Wm. B. Eerdmans, 1959.

BURROWS, M. *The Dead Sea Scrolls.* New York: Viking Press, 1955.

——. *More Light on the Dead Sea Scrolls.* New York: Viking Press, 1958.

CROSS, F. M., Jr. *The Ancient Library of Qumran.* 2nd ed. Garden City: Doubleday Anchor Books, 1961.

DUPONT-SOMMER, A. *The Dead Sea Scrolls: A Preliminary Survey.* Translated by E. Margaret Rowley. Oxford: Basil Blackwell, 1952.

——. *The Essene Writings from Qumran.* Translated by G. Vermès. Oxford: Basil Blackwell, and Cleveland: Meridian Books, 1962.

——. *The Jewish Sect of Qumran and the Essenes: New Studies on the Dead Sea Scrolls.* Translated by R. D. Barnett. New York: Macmillan, 1955.

GASTER, T. H. *The Dead Sea Scrolls in English Translation.* Garden City: Doubleday, 1956 (rev. and enlarged ed., 1964).

MILIK, J. T. *Ten Years of Discovery in the Wilderness of Judaea.* ("Studies in Biblical Theology," No. 26.) Translated by John Strugnell. London: SCM Press, 1959.

RINGGREN, H. *The Faith of Qumran: Theology of the Dead Sea*

Scrolls. Translated by Emilie T. Sander. Philadelphia: Fortress Press, 1963.

ROWLEY, H. H. *From Moses to Qumran. Studies in the Old Testament.* New York: Association Press, 1963.

———. *The Zadokite Fragments and the Dead Sea Scrolls.* Oxford: Basil Blackwell, 1952.

VERMES, G. *The Dead Sea Scrolls in English.* Baltimore: Penguin Books, 1962.

———. *Discovery in the Judean Desert: The Dead Sea Scrolls and Their Meaning.* New York: Desclée, 1957.

YADIN, Y. *The Message of the Scrolls.* New York: Grosset & Dunlap, 1962.

Minor Palestinian Sects and Gnostic Judaism

FRIEDLÄNDER, M. *Der vorchristliche jüdische Gnostizismus.* Göttingen: Vandenhoeck & Ruprecht, 1898.

———. *Die religiösen Bewegungen innerhalb des Judentums im Zeitalter Jesu,* Berlin: G. Reimer, 1905.

GRANT, R. M. *Gnosticism and Early Christianity.* New York: Columbia University Press, 1959.

JONAS, H. *The Gnostic Religion.* 2nd ed., rev.; Boston: Beacon Press, 1963.

KRAELING, C. H. *John the Baptist.* New York: Charles Scribner's Sons, 1951.

SCHOLEM, G. G. *Jewish Gnosticism, Merkabah Mysticism, and Talmudic Tradition.* New York: Jewish Theological Seminary of America, 1960.

———. *On the Kabbalah and its Symbolism.* Translated by Ralph Manheim. London: Routledge and Kegan Paul, 1965.

SCOBIE, C. *John the Baptist.* Philadelphia: Fortress Press, 1964.

STEINMANN, J. *Saint John the Baptist and the Desert Tradition.* Translated by Michael Boyes. New York: Harper & Row, 1958.

THOMAS, J. *Le mouvement baptiste en Palestine et en Syrie.* Gembloux, 1935.

WILSON, R. McL. *The Gnostic Problem. A Study of the Relations between Hellenistic Judaism and the Gnostic Heresy.* London: Mowbray, 1958.

Karaites

WIEDER, N. *The Judean Scrolls and Karaism*. London: East and West Library, 1962.

ZAJACZKOWSKI, A. *Karaism in Poland*. The Hague: Mouton, 1961.

Samaritans

MACDONALD, J. *The Theology of the Samaritans*. ("New Testament Library.") London: SCM Press, and Philadelphia: Westminster Press, 1964 (cf. bibliography, pp. 457-463, for further titles.

Philo and Alexandrian Judaism

BRÉHIER, E. *Les idées philosophiques et religieuses de Philon d'Alexandrie*. 2nd ed.; Paris, 1925.

DANIÉLOU, J. *Philon d'Alexandrie*. Paris, 1957.

GOODENOUGH, E. R. *An Introduction to Philo Judaeus*. New Haven: Yale University Press, 1940, 2nd ed.; Oxford: Basil Blackwell, 1962.

———. *By Light, Light; the Mystic Doctrine of Hellenistic Judaism*. New Haven: Yale University Press, 1935.

SOWERS, S. G. *The Hermeneutics of Philo and Hebrews*. Richmond: John Knox, 1965.

WOLFSON, H. A. *Philo. Foundations of Religious Philosophy in Judaism, Christianity, and Islam*. 2 vols. Cambridge, Mass: Harvard University Press, 1947 (3rd rev. ed., 1962).

Jewish Sects and Primitive Christianity

BLACK, M. *The Scrolls and Christian Origins*. New York: Charles Scribner's Sons, 1956.

CULLMANN, O. *The State in the New Testament.* New York: Charles Scribner's Sons, 1956.

DANIÉLOU, J. *The Dead Sea Scrolls and Primitive Christianity.* Translated by S. Attanasio. Baltimore: Helicon, 1959 (paperback ed.; New American Library, 1962).

HOWLETT, D. *The Essenes and Christianity.* New York: Harper & Row, 1957.

ODEBERG, H. *Pharisaism and Christianity.* Translated by J. M. Moe. St. Louis: Concordia, 1964.

SIMON, M. *St. Stephen and the Hellenists in the Primitive Church.* London and New York: Longmans, Green and Co., 1958.

STAUFFER, E. *Jesus and the Wilderness Community at Qumran.* Translated by Hans Spalteholz. ("Facet Books—Biblical Series," No. 10.) Philadelphia: Fortress Press, 1964.

STENDAHL, K. (ed.). *The Scrolls and the New Testament.* New York: Harper, 1957.

Les manuscrits de la mer Morte. Colloque de Strasbourg, May 25-27, 1955 ("Travaux de centre d'études supérieures spécialisé d'histoire des religions de Strasbourg"). Paris: Presses universitaires de France, 1957.

Indexes

References to Scripture
and Other
Ancient texts

General Index

Abel, 115

Aboth, 35, 36

Abraham, Apocalypse of, 95

Abrahams, I., 135(n.1), 136(n.3)

Acts, Book of, 92, 97-99, 101, 131, 134

Adam, 115, 133

Adonai, 83

After-life, 12, 26-27, 38-39, 79-80

Ain Feshka, 70

Akiba, Rabbi, 38

Alexander Jannaeus, 21, 68 139

Alexander the Great, 2, 108

Allegory, 112-115, 121, 129, 138, **139**

Amme ha aretz, 15

Angels and demons, 27, 39-40, 72, 80-81, 95

Antigonus of Soko, 35

Antioch, 108

Antiochus Epiphanes, 19, 45

Apocrypha, 42 *(See also under names of books)*

"Aaron, Sons of," 71

Aristeas, Letter of, 113, 114, 138, 139

Aristotle, 116

Ark, 128

Athena, 112

Babylonian Exile, 2, 118

Baptism, 72, 75-76, 88-92, 139, 144

Baptists, Contemporary, 5; Jewish sects, 87-92, 96, 107

Bar Cochba, 42, 87

Barnabas, Epistle of, 139

Basanitides, 103

Bene Zadok, See "Zadok, Sons of"

Benediction on the heretics, *See Minim*

Brahmans, 121

Brandon, S.G.F., 137, 137(n.5)

Brownlee, W.H., 51(n.9), 53(n.10), 73(n.19)

Burrows, M., 72(n.18)

Byzantine Age, 54

Cain, 115

Cairo, 53

Caligula, 119

Canaan, 17

Canon, *See* Scripture

Carthage, 108

Christianity, 1, 3, 4, 7, 9, 28, 41, 53, 55-56, 60, 83, 87, 92, 98, 105, 106, 120, 130, chap. 6, *passim (See also* Church)

174

Type, 11 on 13 and 10 on 10 Baskerville
Display, Baskerville
Paper, Spring Grove E. F.